HERBS FOR SALE

Growing and Marketing Herbs, Herbal Products, and Herbal Know-How

Lee Sturdivant

Illustrations by Peggy Sue McRae

A Bootstrap Guide

Published by San Juan Naturals
Friday Harbor, Washington

D0446705

For Tal,
with me every step of the way

Do all your work as though you had
a thousand years to live, and as
you would if you knew you
must die tomorrow.

MOTHER ANN LEE,
SHAKER COMMUNITY FOUNDER

Copyright ©1994 by Lee Sturdivant
All rights reserved. No part of the contents of this book may be reproduced or transmitted in any form or by any means, electronic, photocopying, recording or otherwise, without the written permission of the publisher. For information, contact San Juan Naturals.

PUBLISHED BY:
San Juan Naturals, PO Box 642, Friday Harbor, WA 98250
Printed in the United States of America.

Book design by Words & Deeds, San Jose.

SAN 251-6497

ISBN 0-9621635—2-X
Library of Congress Catalog Card No. 94-065514

10 9 8 7 6 5 4 3

Contents

Herbs and
Small Business

This is a book about herbs, and about small businesses based on herbs. It is written both to honor those who have worked to bring herbs into their rightful place in our lives and homes, and to inspire those who want to consider starting a small business based on these remarkable and useful plants. The major emphasis of the book is on growing and using fresh, organically grown herbs. The book should also interest those who already have a small herb business and might wish to enlarge or change the direction of that business.

The truly ancient appreciation and traditional use of herbs has flourished through all times and throughout the world, almost without exception, until the coming of the modern consumer society in America. The Shaker Communities established wonderfully successful herb companies in eighteenth century America, at least one of which is still open for business today. But after World War II, most Americans only had eyes (and brains) for the future. In a quick turn to the new promise of modern science, everything from the past was suddenly suspect and held in contempt. In with the new, and out with anything to do with the old, the homemade, the nonscientific.

Luckily for us, the herbs themselves remained, along with some few people in this country who continued learning about them, continued using them in many ways. And in other developed countries, especially western Europe, the herbal traditions did not die. Herbal flavorings came again to America's kitchens from Europe after World War II, and from all over the world since then. Herbal products and decorative items are enjoying phenomenal success in the American marketplace as we turn now to more natural, less synthetic materials and goods. And herbal medicines have remained strong in Europe all during the rise of modern western medicine. Today, the pharmacies in Europe still contain shelves of herbal medicine, right alongside the more modern remedies.

Now there is truly an herbal renaissance in America and I write this book in salute to that reassertion of a fine tradition and in the hope of offering a little help to those who would like to be a part of this renewal.

The business of America is business. I never really believed that smug-sounding Calvin Coolidge saying until recently. Now, with the long downturn in the American economy, the lack of decent jobs for even the well educated, and the uptight attitudes that seem to dominate too much of the workplace these days, I am beginning to think that the business of America **has to be** small businesses. And that's the other thing this book is about. The small business potential that's available in the herbal renaissance is real. It's flourishing. It's worth looking into.

My own business experience is limited but genuine. In 1968 I started a boutique for handmade clothing that grew into four retail stores and a manufacturing plant with 125 employees. We made and sold clothing across the country, and during the next seven years my whole family came into the business to save both me and the business, as it grew well beyond my ability to deal with it.

It was not a great success. I always say that it took me about 30 days to get into the garment business and seven years to sell and get out of it. But although I came to dislike the business while waiting for it to sell, I have never regretted it because that experience taught me so much about business and even more about myself, and what I didn't want to do—which was to have such a large business again.

It was a big success in one way, though. In the long days (and nights) of hard work and endurance, my husband and I began dreaming of sailing away from it all. "If we ever get out of this with anything but our skin, let's buy a boat and take the kids and go to sea. Really go to sea. For a long time." Well, that's what we did. Eventually. But that's another story.

That retail, wholesale, and manufacturing business taught us much about the American way of business. Some of those ways have changed, others have not. When I went into business again in the '80s I was determined to operate on a much smaller scale. Since then I have been an herb and flower grower and seller, and a small publisher of books and maps.

This book is an attempt to bring together all of my own small business experiences along with those of people all over the country whose businesses we have visited: herb growers and sellers, large and small; herbal product makers, both beginners and very successful operators; herbal teachers and herbal wildcrafters who run one-person operations or large corporations with sales in the millions; and many different herb farms, those idyllic places where many Americans are getting in touch with herbs and, at the same time, with their own rural roots.

Following each main division of the book is a reference section with recommendations on how to take the next step or get more information about each subject: the books, videos, newsletters, associations, and networks of herb buyers and sellers available in the herbal business world across the country. I hope you'll read the stories of these business people for inspiration and enjoyment and the reference sections to get an idea of just how much good information is out there to help you get into and succeed at whatever you decide to try.

Acknowledgments

IF SOMEONE CAME knocking at my door asking me to take time away from my business so that they could write a book about helping other people get into such a business, I'm not at all sure that I would respond in the gracious and helpful way the people in this book responded to me. My heartfelt thanks and appreciation go out to: Donna and Bill Elliott, Stephenie Caughlin, Eric and Ann Brandt-Meyer, Lois Kenyon, Sally Barksdale, Ernest Pugh, Peter and Nanette Cimino, Mary Preus, Polly & Elliott Haynes, Sheryl and Marshall Lozier, Jim Long, Beth Hailey, Wendy and Jack Newmeyer, Jack Siddall, Brigitte Mars, Tom Pfeiffer, Daniel Gagnon, Al Savinelli, "Brian Horne," Marlin Huffman, Carole Tashel, Kaye Cude, Jürgen and Judith Solie-Engelhardt, and Sue Lukens.

Thanks also, for other special help from: Janet Wright, Louise Dustrude, Steven Foster, Martha Kaye, Rosa Cardini, Ron Engeland, Suzette Mahr, Liz Johnson, and Bruce Conway.

GROWING HERBS

If you grow and sell herbs you will

quickly see that you have become a part of

the intense herbal learning experience

that is going on everywhere.

Growing Culinary Herbs in Your Backyard

L et us begin with one of the easiest and simplest small herb businesses you might want to consider: growing culinary herbs for your local markets and/or restaurants. If you are just learning to grow herbs, this is a good place to start with sales and marketing. This simple backyard herb business is the one I began with years ago. It is also the subject of the first book I ever wrote on growing and marketing (see page 69). I don't intend to repeat that book here, but just to give the barest outlines so that the new reader can know of this easy-start-up business possibility.

With only the smallest of growing areas and quite limited time and money, you can grow culinary herbs for your local grocer or chef. It is relatively easy to earn $50 to $250 a week with this strategy. The assumption here is that you already know how to garden well. If you are a beginning gardener, or have never tried it, you must get those basic skills mastered before being able to earn money at it.

If you've read my other book on herbs, or if you're already past this point in your growing or thinking, then I suggest you skip ahead to the next chapter on Bill Elliott, a much larger herb grower in Denver, Colorado.

My Place, San Juan Island

THIS SIMPLE PLAN for beginners is based on a very basic idea—that your local produce managers and the local chefs in your area need to do the following: #1, provide the freshest product possible to their customers, and #2, keep their waste to a minimum.

Herbs don't ship that well across the country, so locally grown herbs are usually preferred. Because you will be selling to your local stores, you can keep a close eye on freshness for them and make sure your product keeps selling. You can supply herbs from May to October in most areas of the country unless you have a greenhouse, in which case you can supply at least some herbs on an all-year basis.

Here are the varieties and minimum amounts of herbs you need to grow to begin such a small herb business:

BASIL: Grow at least 30 plants to start. Plant two to four times a season.

DILL: Grow at least 20 plants, plant two to four times a season. And, most importantly, make sure it is the ferny or tetraploid dill seeds you grow. Ordinary dill is for pickling and goes quickly to seed. The ferny dill is lush and used for salads, fish, and dips.

FRENCH TARRAGON: Start with six or eight plants. You cannot grow this from seed, and you really can't provide any the first year. Be patient and in two to three years you'll have a lovely tarragon bed that will last at least five more years and earn you some good money every week. Don't waste your time trying Russian tarragon.

MINTS: Start with spearmint (which can be grown from seed) and then find some black peppermint (or other flavorful mints) at a nursery. Grow the different mints apart from each other so they will retain their unusual flavors.

OREGANO: Start with four to six plants of the Greek variety, which is what good cooks love. It has white flowers, while more ordinary oregano has purple blossoms.

SWEET MARJORAM: Six or eight plants will do for this. It needs replanting every year in most areas.

FRENCH SORREL: Start with six plants. It's very hardy.

ROSEMARY: Start with three or four plants and give them winter protection if your temperature drops much below 20°.

CHIVES: Eight or 10 plants to start.

PARSLEY: Six to eight plants to start.

THYME: Start with four or six plants, using the English or Garden variety.

SAGE: Just one or two plants will supply a lot of sage.

These are the basic and best selling herbs in my area, but there are other possibilities you can consider for this little herb growing business: chervil, cilantro, summer savory, fennel, elephant garlic, shallots, lovage, and edible flowers. All can be grown and sold depending on the customers in your local area. If you live in a tropical zone you should also consider growing ginger, roselle, lemon grass, or other tropical herbs. Talk to your local produce managers or chefs to find out what is in demand. Our tastes are becoming much more refined these days as people travel more and are introduced to new flavors everywhere they go. No one had ever heard of lemon grass just a few years ago and now there are Vietnamese restaurants all over the country introducing us to this fine pungent flavor. The plant, by the way, grows easily in my greenhouse—just one tiny plant spread within a year to produce a fine large clump.

One of my best sellers has always been a little packet of mixed herbs: parsley, sage, rosemary, and thyme. I label it Scarborough Mix, after the popular song. It is a good introduction for cooks to the use of culinary herbs.

Even though herbs are becoming more and more popular in the kitchen, there is still much in the way of herb education wanted and needed. Herb books are some of the most popular gardening books on the market, herb classes are well attended all across the country. As I will point out often in this book, America is having a grand love affair with herbs that shows no signs whatsoever of waning. Many, many Americans are still in the first stages of getting to know fresh green herbs in the kitchen. If you grow and sell herbs you will quickly see that you have become a part of this intense herbal learning experience that is going on everywhere. I have grown quite accustomed to being stopped on the street in my community to be asked about a certain herb—where to find it, how to grow it, how to use it.

Edible flowers are another product I have sold along with herbs. These blossoms are still in demand in some areas around the country, but I do notice they are becoming less popular in restaurants. Just be prepared to grow them if asked by a local chef—they still make a delightful garnish. The most popular blossoms (and easiest to grow) are nasturtiums, borage, calendulas, pansies and violas, lemon marigold, and squash blossoms. I give a much longer list in my first herb book (written when edible flowers were all the rage) plus a list of toxic blossoms. I do firmly suggest that if you get into growing edible blossoms, you learn just what is safe and what isn't.

Toxicity is a subject all herbalists need to take very seriously. In our urge to tell the world about the wonderful properties of herbs, we shouldn't ignore the fact that some of those herbs and flowers can be slightly toxic or even very dangerous. As you begin to take part in the growing American return to herbalism, it will become apparent to you how important it is that we stress knowledge and reasonableness.

The other product that I have had good luck with is what I call a European Salad Mix—which is becoming an excellent product for many small growers around the country. It is often sold as Wild and Seasonal Salad or as Mesclun.

Larousse, the gourmet resource, defines mesclun as "a mixture of young shoots and leaves of wild plants used to make a salad." Today it has become a combination of varied and colorful salad greens combined with an assortment of flavorful culinary herbs. It makes an outstanding salad and sells for up to eight dollars per pound in the markets in my area—for less in other areas. Chefs also pay dearly for bags full of this mix that are carefully washed and dried and ready to serve. I describe this product in some detail in a later chapter in this section about Seabreeze Organic Farm.

SO NOW YOU have a backyard full of lush growing green herbs—at least four popular culinary herbs in large enough quantities to supply them for the whole growing season. Who will be interested in paying you for them? Two of the best customers for a small grower are local supermarkets and local chefs. I don't mean Safeway® or someone that large—although they certainly sell lots of green herbs these days, and you'll learn more about that kind of marketing in the next chapter on Elliott Gardens. What you need to find at first is an independent, full service market that caters to good cooks. It probably has a deli, gourmet coffee that customers can grind to suit their taste, an extensive variety of vegetables and fruit—I think you know the type I mean. If they aren't yet selling fresh green herbs OR if they are selling herbs from thousands of miles away, they will probably be interested in talking to you about supplying them with your home-grown product.

What follows now is almost verbatim from my other book—sales and marketing tips that can be important to your success. This is the key that worked for me and that can help you unlock the door to your first sales. Many of us seem to have a love-hate relationship with even the word, S.A.L.E.S. In this country, it seems, we are much better trained to buy things than to sell them. But if you are seriously considering becoming a small grower or a small business person, sales of your product must be just as important in your mind as producing the product itself, at least until you figure out how to market well what you've grown or made.

Many people imagine there's an impossibly high wall between what goes on in the front of a grocery store and what goes on in the back, where they never feel welcome. The people who *are* welcome in the back of the store are the people with something good to sell. And that's what you'll have with fresh green herb packets.

After you have picked out your first market to try, find out the produce buyer's name and the hours during which he can be seen. You can get that information at the store or from home on the phone. Make an early morning appointment to see him to show "a locally grown product I know you'll like." Be sure to take some packets of herbs when you go in.

The produce buyer is most interested in a few things when considering a new product: having a good selection of produce to keep the customers coming in, and making a decent profit on it without a big loss in unsold waste. You must now offer all of the above with the following spiel.

"I grow these kitchen herbs in my backyard. I'm prepared to keep you supplied in fresh culinary herbs, take back any packets that don't sell, and try to meet any special needs your customers might have.

"I get $1.25 for each packet that sells. Most stores charge $1.79 or $1.89 for the packet, and I can bill you weekly or monthly.

"I'll check the display at least twice a week. I'm reliable and eager to make my little herb business grow."

That's the basic information you need to get across. Read it over and over until you know exactly what to say. Be straightforward and good humored and don't waste the produce manager's time with small talk. You'll have a chance to get acquainted later as you do business there. Produce people are very, very busy in the best markets and will expect you to be businesslike in dealing with them. I should note that in my first book I set the herb packet price at only one dollar, but with increasing prices since I wrote that, I now think $1.25 is a more realistic price.

This basic spiel is really all the selling you have to do to get into the herb business. If you've chosen the right market, you'll find that getting the account is not a problem. Produce people these days know that herbs are becoming big business because their customers are asking for them.

Now let's take a look at just what you've offered and are asking for in return.

First of all, you're not asking for an order for so many packets of such and such an herb. That's not the best way for a backyard grower to begin to market herbs. You want to keep as much control as possible in this little business and that means being able to sell just what you have that's ready to harvest. In most weather zones, or with a greenhouse, you can supply some herbs from May to October, but not all varieties that whole time. In some zones you can supply almost all year round. These days your sales will always be highest during the basil season, but other herbs, like dill and tarragon for instance, are becoming very, very popular, too. The Scarborough Mix will sell well anytime.

What you're actually wanting is to rent a tiny little space on your greengrocer's refrigerated counter where you can keep the market supplied with something they and their customers want. By offering to take back any packets that don't sell, you can also control your sales because you'll know exactly what to offer the customers and can monitor the sales very well. Often grocers can order the "wrong" items. Then, when they don't sell, the grocer takes the loss and the supplier doesn't get any more business. You can take the first losses, learn from your customers and continue to supply what they want. This point is very important. You want to decide exactly what to bring into the market. Your first year or two in business you probably won't have a complete selection all the time.

The mark-up you've suggested is really quite good, but your grocer is free to mark it up higher if he wants to—he knows what his customers will pay. The $1.25 to you should remain steady.

A basket of herbs in the market always looks inviting.

That's what makes all the work worthwhile.

After the grocer agrees to try your herbs:

1) Take in at least 15 or 20 packets for your first delivery.

2) Take your first order in in a nice basket. If the store doesn't have a small tray for the refrigerated counter, you can leave the basket. Herbs look great and sell well from a basket; just **make sure it stays in the refrigerated section.**

3) Take along a small sign: "Local Fresh Herbs." You can attach it to the basket or the display until the market gets around to making its own. Make sure your sign is waterproof: water sprays are often used over the whole refrigerated section.

4) Offer to price your own packets. Sometimes a store will appreciate the help in marking; other stores will just have you leave the herbs in the back until an employee has time to mark them.

5) Be certain to have an employee sign for each delivery. More about that in a bit.

6) To start with, keep a separate tally for yourself of just what you take in so that you can learn what's selling the fastest. Bring in not less than six packets of herbs per delivery.

Remove any packets that start looking unappetizing. If the herbs are harvested and packaged correctly, and then **kept in the refrigerated section**, they should all hold up fine for about a week—some for much longer. The better and fresher they look, the faster they will sell.

Don't get discouraged if the sales are slow to start. Customers have to get used to seeing a new vegetable or fruit or greens. You may even lose money for the first few weeks the first season— but if you've chosen the right store and grown fine herbs, you'll soon start selling lots of packets and decide it's time to look for a second account. Be certain your garden will produce enough now to more than double your sales. It may be you'll want to stay with just one market the first season, until your garden is producing more.

Now what about supplying your local branch of a chain store supermarket? Yes, you should definitely consider this, especially if there are no good local-owner stores in your area, and if the chain store isn't already carrying herbs. But your sales method may have to be quite different. Many, but not all, large chains forbid their store produce managers to buy local crops. Your produce manager will tell you this when you go in to see him. But show him your packets and ask if he'd like to carry them if you go to the trouble of going to the main office, and if the main office will allow him to purchase your herbs if you clear it first with them. If he's interested, it may be worth your while to go further. Those buying offices may be a long way away, even a hundred miles or so. I've never felt the additional expense would be worth it. It has always seemed easier to look a little further for small specialty stores, delis, co-ops, locally owned grocers. While your first herb crops are growing, take the time to find just the right account.

RESTAURANTS ARE ANOTHER golden opportunity for a back-yard herb dealer. Their herb usage grows yearly. In a recent (January 1993) poll done by *The Business of Herbs*, weekly

INVOICE NO.
5256

SHIPPED TO			
	STREET & NO.		
SOLD TO		STATE	ZIP
NO.	ZIP	CITY	
		DATE	

SAN JUAN NATURALS
P.O. BOX 642
FRIDAY HARBOR, WA 98250
(206) 378-2648
FAX (206) 378-2584

INVOICE NO.
5263

INVOICE

SOLD TO			SHIPPED TO		
KING'S MARKET					
STREET & NO. SPRING S.—			STREET & NO.		
CITY FRIDAY HARBOR	STATE WA	ZIP 98250	CITY	STATE	ZIP

CUSTOMER'S ORDER	SALESMAN	TERMS NET 10 DAYS	F.O.B.	DATE		
9/21	18 PKTS			1	25	22 50
9/27	24 PKTS			1	25	30 00
9/28	17 PKTS			1	25	21 25
10/1	25 PKTS			1	25	31 25
						105 00

REDIFORM
7L721/
01723

Here's an example of a simple invoice for one store account.
Use a rubber stamp at the top. Using one line per delivery,
you can do six or eight deliveries on one invoice.

consumption by their surveyed restaurants averaged 10 pounds of herbs per week. The most commonly purchased herbs in those restaurants were: basil, thyme, cilantro, rosemary, parsley, mint, tarragon, dill, oregano, and chives, in descending order.

Pick out the gourmet restaurants in your area or, more to the point, those restaurants that feature lots of fresh vegetables, specialty salads, homemade soups and breads.

By phone you can find out the name of the chef and what time she comes to work. Try to see her as early in the day as possible. Like the greengrocer, chefs are very busy people. Use the same type of spiel you do for markets, but of course chefs won't be reselling your packets directly. Take in two or three packets to start, keep your price at $1.25, leave the packets with her to try (no charge) and call back in a day or two to see if you can do business there.

You may find that one or two restaurants plus one good market account can use up your fresh herb supply quite nicely, especially the first year or two. After your garden is well established and you know just what to expect from your plants (and have probably added to your inventory based on your own sales) you can reach out to other new accounts.

My other book on herbs gives quite a few details on billing, credit, taxes, and so forth. And those subjects are covered throughout this book, in relation to other herb businesses. You can use the simplest of bookkeeping methods by using duplicate invoices to bill your accounts, with the second copy as your monthly and year-end sales record. Just be certain that you get someone in the store or restaurant to sign for each shipment of herbs you make. I use one invoice for several deliveries to a single store, listing each delivery on one line. When you remove any herb packets, you also need to make that note on the invoice and deduct for that packet(s).

As all gardeners know only too well, many expenses are incurred in keeping up a garden of any kind, and almost all of these can be charged off against an herb business you run from that garden. Just remember that the Internal Revenue Service doesn't consider it a legitimate home business if it **never** earns a profit.

You can use zip-lock bags for your herbs, as some growers do, but I have always used 2x4x12" clear plastic bags that are labeled as **1 quart capacity** and are **.95 mil** thick. They cost about two to three cents each in cartons of 50 or a hundred, and I leave the tops open so that customers can smell the herbs. I would recommend that you use zip-lock bags for selling the salad mixes as so many small leaves can easily be spilled from an open bag.

I am a firm believer in keeping your expenses low the first year or so in order to deal with the learning experience itself. If this is your first business venture, you may well go through several mind changes about about what it is you are doing. And you may find that this kind of self-motivated endeavor is really not for you. Why have a box full of expensive, fancy labels or packaging left over should you decide to drop the idea partway through your first year? The crack and peel labels I began using after the first year or so of sales are quite nice, and easy to deal with. But they are expensive—especially if they just end up sitting on the shelf. Yes, nice labels will increase your sales, but they are a big start-up expense and not necessary in the beginning.

Instead, I recommend that you start with a package of stick-on labels from the local stationery store measuring approximately 2½"x3" or 3"x4". These will cost you two or three cents each. You also need a rubber stamp with your company name, address and (usually) phone number on it. Use a little creative design on these packet labels, if you like, but legally they only require the name of the herb plus your name and address. Make your labels and stick them onto the bags just before you harvest. Write the herb name on the label before you fill the bag. Be sure to use a waterproof pen.

I didn't use a weight or volume measure on the labels simply because the cost of a commercial scale was too high for me when I first began. My markets did not demand that the weight be listed on the label. I chose instead to go with a "customer's eye" method that stood me in good stead all along. I put enough in the bags so that I, as a customer, would feel it was good value

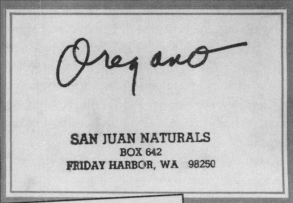

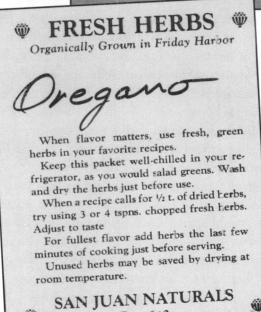

*The plain label can also be jazzed up with rubber
stamps, stickers, or art work. The printed label is
called "crack and peel." Be sure to use a waterproof
pen on both kinds of labels.*

were I purchasing this little herb packet myself. I always look at herb offerings in every market I go into, so I know how my product stacks up with the competition. When herbs are growing well, they produce lots and lots of pickable harvest. Be generous in your packaging and you'll never hear any complaints. If you're too skimpy, your sales will drop off. I resent finding tiny little scraps of herbs for sale at high prices, and would refuse to buy them.

Every week or so give the market the original invoice for the signed deliveries and they will pay you very quickly—often while you wait a few minutes. Markets are used to dealing in cash and will understand that you can't give long credit terms for such a small business. Credit is another issue that will come up often in this book, but in this instance you will be operating on such a small scale to begin with that the longest credit you should consider giving to an account is 10 days. And no discounts. On every invoice form there is a box for the "terms" of the sale you are making: when the bill is due and what discounts are offered for timely payment. I suggest you write "net 10 days" on that line which means the whole bill is due within 10 days.

If you are dealing with a store where a weight measurement is demanded, you will have to go to a little more trouble. In that case, I would use a little Weight Watcher™ or postage scale and always add a little extra herb. You won't get in trouble if you supply more than the weight you claim—only if you supply less.

Never pick wet herbs, and don't wash them after they are picked. Herbs combined with water in plastic equal quick rotting. You need to put dry herbs in the plastic bags. Also, herbs should be **organically grown**—you should **never use pesticides** on them. I often see customers pick off a tiny leaf from inside an herb packet in the market and take a little taste. Herbs are for flavor and good cooks want to know if your herbs deliver that flavor. Don't deliver pesticides or herbicides to them instead. Besides, herbs are tough, ancient plants and are seldom bothered by pests.

(Yes, it could happen that some late spring morning the aphids find your dill bed before the ladybugs find the aphids. In that case you would have to wash the dill in cold water before you can deliver it to market. No big deal. Just use a salad spinner and dry the herbs thoroughly before you put them in the plastic bag.)

Here are some harvesting hints for each of the main culinary herbs, plus an approximate amount and weight for the amount of herb you should pick for each one. These depend a lot on the size of your plants. I have always tended to put more in my packets than many suppliers do. That's certainly not necessary. Except for the chives, I pick the herbs by pinching them off using just the ends of my forefinger and thumb.

BASIL. Don't let these plants go to flower. That stops their leaf production. Ten to 15 basil stems (depending on the leaf size) should make a full looking bag and weigh in at about 2½ ounces.

DILL. Ten to 12 stems of this ferny dill should weigh about 1½ ounces and make a fine packet. With very young plants, up to 15 stems may be needed.

FRENCH TARRAGON. Ten to 12 stems make a fine packet.and will weigh about 1½ ounces.

SCARBOROUGH MIX. Four or five fluffy sprigs of curly parsley, three or four stems of sage, three or four stems of thyme leaves (and flowers), and two or three stems of rosemary make a fragrant packet of useful herbs that many people will buy.

MINT. Use 15 or even 20 stems here. You will always have lots of mint to use. It will weigh 2+ ounces. If you use mixed varieties just mark the bag as Mints.

OREGANO. Twelve to 15 stems will do here, weighing approximately 1½ ounces. Include a few flower stems if there are some.

MARJORAM. Harvest the same as oregano and in about the same quantities. Add flower stems if available.

FRENCH SORREL. Be certain to keep the flower stems cut off on this plant. Don't let them flower at all. A bag full of sorrel may weigh up to three ounces or more, but it takes quite a bit to make sorrel soup, one of the most popular uses for this herb.

ROSEMARY. Eight to 10 stems will weigh about an ounce or a little more, but that is a lot of rosemary—a strongly flavored, little-goes-a-long-way herb.

CHIVES. Grasp a small (1½" to 2") bunch. Cut them off with a knife or scissors near the base of the plant. The packet will weigh about 3 ounces. Each bunch will be clean for the first few cuttings, and then the bunches will need cleaning to remove the stiff flower stems, weeds, etc. To clean them easily, hold the bunch close to the tips and shake out the messy bits. Be sure to include a flower stem or two in each packet when they are available.

THYME. Try 10 to 15 stems—about an ounce of herb. I always try to package only the tender green stems—not the woody ones. It is fine to include flowers with this one.

SAGE. Never a best seller for me except during the holidays (sage produces almost all year long in my area) but it is necessary for the Scarborough Mix. The packet should weigh about 2 ounces—about 15 stem tips make a nice packet.

This little backyard herb business can grow to something much larger, of course, if you simply keep adding new accounts to your sales efforts and new herb production to your garden. After I got my herb production fairly high, I began supplying a restaurant distributor, one who delivers supplies to restaurants several times a week in a large geographical area. And that brings us to describing a much different level of fresh cut culinary herb production such as occurs near Denver, Colorado, at Elliott Gardens.

Elliott Gardens, Denver

BILL AND DONNA Elliott were raised in families who have been
growing carnations for the flower market since the 1940s. They
have grown carnations themselves in covered greenhouses for all
of their married life. They live now on the outskirts of Denver,
Colorado.

Over the last 20 years or so the carnation business, like many
other flower businesses, has moved almost completely to South
America, where land and labor are much, much cheaper. Over
the last 10 years the Elliotts have moved almost completely into
the growing of culinary herbs.

One of their mini-carnation customers was a large restaurant
distributor who repeatedly asked the Elliotts to look into growing herbs. Bill and Donna could find almost no cultural information on commercial herb growing and set about to learn on
their own. Today they sell a steady **300 pounds of culinary herbs
per day,** all year long, and grow most of them in a little more
than one acre of greenhouses.

On the remaining part of their two acres, Bill and Donna also
have their home, a fairly large retail shop area, two large coolers,
a packaging area, and some remaining beds of long-stemmed
carnations because "we just can't give them up completely."

The original carnation beds—raised, redwood boxes, six
inches deep and still filled with the original four or five inches of
"the best topsoil imaginable from Table Mountain at Golden,
Colorado"—now grow all the herbs. Bill steam sterilizes the soil
at 180° to get rid of weed seeds and uses inexpensive tape hoses
on top of the dirt for drip irrigation . The original gate irrigation
system used for the carnations wouldn't work for the herbs, Bill
says. "You can't spray water on the herb foliage because it gets
ruined. That's all there is to it. You have to keep the herbs dry."

Herb greenhouse,
Elliott Gardens

One other major difference for the Elliotts in switching to growing herbs meant switching away from pesticides and becoming an organic grower of food. Growing under glass means dealing with an unnatural environment where bug control can become just as important as plant production. The major bug problem at the Elliotts' operation is white flies and their method of dealing with them is what Bill calls "dry cleaning": cutting a bunch of herbs and then shaking them sharply to remove the flies. It may sound a little silly, but it looks to be remarkably effective in the demonstration he gives us. "If you grow herbs inside," says Bill, "you are going to have white flies on at least one or two of the herbs, period. You can't do a thing about it. At least we can't. We've tried all the exotic methods, and they haven't worked. Now, we just do this dry cleaning and shake them off. We try never, ever to wash the herbs."

For popular herbs like tetraploid dill, they keep several beds going at a time.

"Here's today's harvesting bed we can use for the next week or so, here's one coming along just behind that, and here's one planted just three days ago."

They also sell a lot of cilantro, getting three or four cuts per bed in the fall, winter and spring, but only one cut per bed in the summer before it goes to seed. Cilantro is a very popular herb for both Asian and Hispanic market areas.

At least a third of one large greenhouse is devoted to edible flowers, a product Bill thinks is **not** going out of style very soon. Dianthus, nasturtiums, and marigolds were the main flower blossoms at the time of our visit.

Harvesting of the herbs is done with ordinary hand grass clippers because the angle is right for the cuts and large cuts can be done at once. The herbs are collected in early morning in foam boxes (which can often sit atop the plants) and taken to the coolers. The herb cooler is kept at 50°, the flower cooler at 34° to 35°. "If we put the herbs in the colder flower cooler," says Bill, "they'll look just beautiful for awhile and then simply collapse from tissue damage."

Elliott Gardens is strictly a family operation. Bill and Donna, their grown children, and one or two other members of the family are all part of the labor force. As the children start to raise their own families the pressure stays on the operation to keep growing larger and larger to support more and more people. The property doesn't grow, the pressure on it does.

Much of the Elliott herb effort has been made in getting to the right sales level with a minimum of extra costs. Right now they have three basic customers: Safeway® markets in the Denver region, and two large restaurant distributors who supply the chefs and a few of the smaller markets in the area. Getting to this point has taken much trial and error, "and a lot of herb dumping," says Bill, as they worked through problems of delivery, packaging, and just which herbs to supply.

Safeway® came to them several years ago in response to their own customer demand for herbs. "It was a really big deal for us then," says Bill, "but it quickly became a big mess. We didn't know enough about what we were doing then and, more importantly, neither did they. There was so much waste. And the wrong packaging. No one knew how to take care of the herbs. If we took them in in bunches they got too dried out. If they were put into water they either ran out of water and got dried out or they got too soaked in water. They didn't know what to order. After a few weeks, we all just gave up." Safeway® and Elliott Gardens both lost money.

Then a few things happened that changed the picture completely. Bar-coding came in, for one thing. That's the system even small markets are installing now that allows a store clerk to simply pass the coded product lightly over an infra-red scanning system at the checkout counter. That records the sale at the sales point and also puts the sale into inventory and marketing systems in the same computer system.

During that period, Elliott himself "set out to learn much more about herbs." He read a lot, talked to everyone he could to get more information, and prepared himself for what he thought would be another try to put his herbs into a larger market. The Safeway® people returned in about a year. They worked through the problems again and the two businesses have worked well together ever since.

Nowadays, every Safeway® in the area records their herb (and all) sales automatically on the scanning system. The information is collected every day through the central offices, and the next day's herb order is prepared and called in to Elliott. His own labels are now bar coded so that the type of herb being sold at the store is registered at each sale. This Universal Product Code (UPC) for food products is part of a fairly expensive system—not something a small grower would ever consider. But for the Elliotts it has been the answer to ever growing sales.

After several different packaging attempts the Elliotts have settled on a small, clear, rigid plastic box that holds one ounce of any herb. The Elliott Gardens' crack and peel label is stuck onto the box by Donna's aunt who also helps out at the greenhouse.

The UPC code on each box tells which herb it is. The whole-sale price on the herbs varies, but is usually close to a dollar a packet.

Bill says he can anticipate the orders pretty well now. There is always more basil wanted than anything else—three to one. In the early days basil was a big problem, when they tried hard to grow it through the winter. Now Bill imports basil from Hawaii in the winter, and tarragon from New Zealand, so that he can provide all of his fresh herbs all year long, and protect his customer base. (The tarragon beds in his greenhouse go dormant every winter, but the imports keep it selling.) He has tried importing basil from Israel and California but gets the best year-round product from Hawaii. A few years ago he had to pay up to $16 a pound for basil. Now he finds he can consistently get it for around $3 a pound.

He's also working on a way to market mint marigold *(Tagetes lucida)* as a winter substitute for tarragon. Many chefs around the country are substituting this herb in the winter for tarragon, but retail customers haven't learned much about it yet.

Besides the Safeway® account, which must be taken care of daily, Elliott Gardens also serves two large food distributors, who in turn deliver to most of the restaurants in the area. Bill has settled on two sizes for them: one pound packages, and four ounce packs. He says he cannot afford to deliver to smaller markets or other accounts, because of the high transportation costs.

The herb production has become a neat, seemingly slick system of herb growing and sales. The labor is done primarily by family members plus occasional help from others. The Elliotts never have to worry about not being paid, or looking for new customers all the time. With only three customers their book-keeping is incredibly easy. Over the years they have also found a few specialty accounts around the country, who will take any extra herb product they happen to have.

"It's handy," says Bill, "to have a few places who will take any extra crop we grow, so we don't have to leave it on the plant.

When it's ready to harvest we need to harvest it. " He tries to keep his own prices steady all year at $3.75 for a four ounce package.

Bill doesn't think the herb business is letting up at all—but is still on the upswing. "Every town," he says, "can have their own little guy to grow herbs because they can be so fresh. California is always after my customers here but they can't touch me on freshness. They can certainly price me out because they can grow things cheaper there, but they just can't touch me on freshness, which is becoming more and more important all the time."

Although his system seems almost foolproof, Elliott seems to be something of a natural worrier. And his own special situation of small acreage that constantly needs to produce more and more, makes him continue to look at new possibilities. He is considering looking for one more big herb account and trying to figure out the space for that. He is talking with people from Jamaica who want to grow for him. "They love to grow," says Bill, "but they don't want to do the marketing. We're going to try a few herbs with them. Maybe even get into ginger." He's gone to Hawaii and Phoenix looking for land, wondering if he should move.

Meanwhile, instead of just re-opening the retail area in the spring (where they usually sell herb and vegetable starts to people in the area) they are preparing for a grand opening to turn it into a year-round retail shop. Family members are making crafts, one has long made and sold pies. They'll bring in some Christmas trees and poinsettias. The ideas are plentiful.

"My kids just can't work for allowances anymore. They're starting their own families now. We've got to look ahead to the future. If herbs ease up, I'll find something else to grow. Or some other place to grow them."

He's not too open to the idea of trying new culinary herb varieties anymore. "I went to one of those herb conferences and someone suggested epazote (*Chenopodium ambrosioides*)—that was going to be a big deal. So I planted it, but I couldn't sell **any** of it and it's still sprouting up in this greenhouse all over the place, every single year."

He stays with the basic herbs but looks every day, thinks every day, wonders every day how to get his tiny acreage to pay more. Denver is sprawling out to meet him, making his land more valuable as land, but it produces so well for him that selling the land seems foolish. Right now he is trying a few baby vegetables for someone, wondering if that could pay as well as herbs, scratching his head, wondering how to get a firm handle on the future and hold on to it.

Seabreeze Organic Farm, Southern California

"THIS IS MY Tara. I'll do anything to stay on this land," says Stephenie Caughlin, standing on the hilltop behind Del Mar, California, looking out towards Torrey Pines State Park and the blue Pacific surf.

Her 1.8 acres of sea-view hilltop are tightly terraced and planted in rows and rows of herbs and greens. Nearby another 1.75 acres of leased land is planted in specialty vegetables. Seabreeze Organic Farm grows specialty greens for seven different Southern California farmers' markets. Stephenie, or one of her employees, goes out in her pickup truck every Sunday, Tuesday, and Thursday, plus twice on Wednesdays and Saturdays, to set up at the public farmers' markets now being run in most areas of San Diego County.

She brings tables, a shade tent, plastic bags, signs, a cash box, large wax-treated boxes full of greens, and lots of sun block, as she proceeds to sell what she's picked early, early that morning or late the evening before.

Her best selling product, and the one we are most interested in, is the mixed greens that are called European Salad Mix, Wild and Seasonal Salad Mix, or often, Mesclun. Stephenie calls hers Country Salad Mix. The original name of Mesclun implies only tiny or baby greens and Stephenie has learned that more flavor and nutrition comes from greens that are allowed to grow a little larger.

These salad mixes, which originated in the south of France, are starting to appear across the country on many fancy restaurant menus, and in many markets that cater to gourmet or health food cooks. They are a mix of greens, herbs, and often edible flowers, served together on a salad plate with vinaigrette, sometimes with walnuts or a little goat's milk cheese added. The mix

Today's best salads are full of unusual greens, herbs, and edible flowers.

generally contains unusual greens, some of them very full-flavored—even slightly bitter. When combined with snippets of green herbs and flowers, the taste of ordinary green salads gives way to a full-bodied, interesting, truly delicious combination of tastes that can be fabulous. (Yep, I love 'em.)

In my area these mixed greens sell for up to eight dollars a pound, depending on the market, and restaurant chefs pay dearly for them if they are delivered washed, dried and table ready. Of course, as more and more growers get into supplying these salad mixes, we can expect the prices to decrease. But if they are not yet available in your area, this is a product to consider.

Stephenie sells her mixes at six dollars per pound, or three dollars for a half pound at the farmers' markets and says there is too much competition in the area to get any more for them. Even so, she manages to sell hundreds of pounds of the mix per week along with a thousand or so heads of unusual lettuces. Recently, she added a combination of cooking greens that she also sells for six dollars per pound. These are becoming popular now for both quick stir-frying or cooking in the longer, more old-fashioned way. These can include collards, kale, bok choy, and turnip greens.

Taste really is the important factor in this business. The customers Caughlin gets at the markets come back every week to buy from her, even though cheaper greens and lettuces are available to them all week, everywhere. They are willing to pay her higher prices because of the flavor these salad mixes deliver. And the flavors are a direct result of the years Stephenie has spent growing seeds from all over the world, to see just what will grow the best in her soil and develop outstanding flavors.

We stop to taste at every bed we pass on the hillside. Incredible. Most mesclun, she says, has too many baby greens in the mix—"they really don't have the flavor." She lets her plants mature more and then, if the leaves are too large, simply cuts them before adding to the mix. "The important thing is the flavor, not the look."

Stephenie uses up to 26 ingredients. In the winter, she says, the special flavors might come from claytonia and mâche. In summer, amaranth lends a special flavor. Plus all the sweet specialty lettuces, plus arrugula, raddichio, fennel, golden purslane, dill, cilantro, parsley and... "I've got to keep some of this secret," she laughs, and stops the list mid-stream.

She has just put in a large bed of flowers for cutting. "I've finally noticed," she says, "that people really will feed their souls first. And pay plenty for it, too. You can't believe how many times someone will walk up to our stand with $25 worth of cut flowers in their arms and ask me how much I'm charging for a head of lettuce! So I've decided to join them. At least a little."

Caughlin takes the organic part of the growing very seriously. For fertilizer, she raises a hundred chickens (Missouri Wonders, Arucanas and Rhode Island Reds), and sells their multi-colored eggs for $4 per dozen at the markets. She collects horse manure from the local horse ranches in nearby Rancho Santa Fe ("the best fed, best cared for horses in the country"), and refuses to use steer manure because of the saline content and the possible use of chemicals and growth hormones in their feed. She raises zillions of earthworms and frogs (to help with insect problems) and battles constantly with the California government agents about their "expensive, bungling, bureaucratic" organic certification program.

She wishes every day that more people could learn how much better it is to eat organically grown foods instead of all the vegetables and greens now being brought in from other countries where there are few limits on the amounts and types of pesticides and herbicides that can be used on crops.

"Just look at the gloves all the produce workers are wearing now in the supermarkets around here," she says. "Do you think those gloves are there to protect the workers from the customers? No way. It's because of the chemicals on the product. But people just don't get it."

Her watering is by drip tape hoses on timers. The cutting of the greens is done with a seven inch stainless steel knife, and many of the crops for the salad mix are "cut and come again" varieties from which she can get three crops before replanting.

After cutting, the greens are taken to a 15'x25' shelter with stainless steel tables and large draining racks using grocery store delivery bread racks. The washing is done on the tables with hoses. There's also one large tub used for any root vegetables that need a little soaking. All of the water is recycled into the garden.

One big but very necessary expense was for a large walk-in cooler that holds the heavy waxed boxes of vegetables, greens, and herbs after they are cut and washed. Each box is carefully labeled with the contents and the market it is destined for.

Expenses are starting to get Stephenie down and, with another staggering 24 percent increase in her water bills coming this year, she is beginning to wonder if she can make it on this expensive land. Southern California is not yet out of the biggest depression to hit there since the '30s, with more military bases still to be closed, more defense plants still downsizing or disappearing altogether. The state is still floundering in unemployment as we meet. Seabreeze Organic Farm overlooks some of the most expensive real estate in the world, but the population in the area is full of the uncertainty and caution that comes from economic hard times. These are real restraints on her ability to raise prices to meet her own increasing expenses.

Stephenie Caughlin used to be a school teacher in La Jolla.

One day in the '70s she stumbled onto the property she now stands on and simply fell in love with it. She gave up her teaching job and became first a mortgage broker and then a commodities broker, working in offices in Chicago and Newport Beach. Stephenie was very successful, eventually opening her own office and living the fast California good life. But the stress was incredible, and she began to realize that what had really drawn her to the piece of land near the coast was that it represented what she remembered as the best of California as a child. It is still almost rural, still full of wildlife, still unspoiled and beautiful. Being inside all day in a brokerage office was hardly the way to enjoy that land. And her own growing environmental awareness made her start to question the life she was leading As a broker, she says, "there's an image you need to project, with expensive cars, expensive meals, and expensive clothing. I just couldn't keep that up and keep square with my own ideas.

"After a while, all I wanted to do was be outside all day—every day. I began to spend too much time staring out the window at cloud formations. Finally, I decided to try this and, frankly, I still don't know if I can make it. Now there is getting to be a lot of stress at this, what with all the increasing costs and the poor economy. I really can't predict whether I'll be able to make it at this."

Once an area becomes fancy real estate, any kind of farming is almost out of the question, if your expenses have to include land payments. And the area around Del Mar, California, is almost beyond fancy real estate. Very nice, very livable homes on quarter acre lots there are purchased at $800,000, or more, and simply torn down the very next day to make room for $2,000,000 homes that someone will purchase, just to be in such a lovely area with such a high image address. Incredibly, the poor economy is not really bringing land prices in that specific area down very much. Everything seems to be on hold waiting for the next boom.

But Stephenie is not a gal to give up very easily. "Here, taste these Market Express turnips. That seed costs $90 a pound, but they're tastier than apples. And my customers do love them. How about this French Batavia lettuce, isn't that a flavor? And it will hold up under a Caesar dressing, too."

The breeze from the sea cools us as we walk along the terraced hillside, the quiet clucking of the hens is soothing in the late spring afternoon. In the distance, the distinctive torrey pine silhouette frames the rolling surf. It reminds me of an earlier, easier time in this golden state of opportunity. It's simply too beautiful here to really worry for very long. Maybe everything is still possible here. Yes, it probably is. And, if that is so, then Seabreeze Organic Farm will do just fine.

Good Earth Farm, Maine

FROM THESE RELATIVELY simple herb growing operations I'd like to take the reader now to something (and someplace) entirely different. Freeport, Maine, to be exact, and the Good Earth Farm of Eric and Ann Brandt-Meyer.

These young, hardworking people grow lots of herbs along with fields of flowers for the decorative market. They are one of perhaps 20 or 30 fairly large dried flower growers in the country who supply the thousands of retail accounts where bunches of dried herbs and flowers are sold. Many of the zillions of wreaths and swags available in retail shops in every village, town, and city in the country begin in the flower fields of the Good Earth Farm.

Our visit to the farm comes toward the end of harvest season, the middle of the main shipping season. The loft of the big barn is stuffed with bunches of herbs and flowers drying in the fan-made breezes. The barn floors are covered with huge piles of Sweet Annie, hurriedly thrown inside because of an early frost— "our version of a hurricane," says Eric. Employees, piles and piles of dried flower bunches, shipping cartons, tractors, and giant clumps of pumpkins are everywhere; so are cats and dogs and children. It's only nine or ten in the morning and already families are arriving to take hayrides into the fields to pick out their Halloween pumpkins—one of the farm's autumn offerings to locals.

Walking around the barnyard, listening to the pleasant murmur of the employees inside, the chickens nearby, the children on the tractor in the fields, I soon recognize that feeling I get fairly often when visiting small growers around the country: these people are here because this is still the place for a very good life. As the great migration from rural areas to town and suburb continues in this country, some few are recognizing that the better life for families is still to be had in small towns or on acreage. The challenge is in figuring out a way to stay on the land and earn a decent living.

For Eric, a friendly, articulate college history major from northern Virginia, that first effort at making it on the land was to grow and sell vegetables at a vegetable stand. That was tough, he says, and he soon "grew tired of throwing away bushels of beans." He eventually responded to "requests from customers and florist shops to start growing flowers." He quickly recognized dried flowers as a relatively value-added product, and soon added dried herb bunches—again in response to demand from his customers. Besides two dozen varieties of dried flowers, he also sells dried two ounce bunches of anise hyssop, dill, lemon mint, marjoram, oregano, purple basil, thyme, sage, and savory, all for about $3 per bunch.

Eric's experience is, I think, quite typical of those who change from roadside stands, where you deal directly with your retail customers, to a wholesale business. The choices he has had to make are those any grower has to make once they choose the path of selling to lots of individual shops. He ships his product by United Parcel Service all over the east coast, selling to hundreds of different florist and store accounts.

When that is the course your business takes, one of the first and most important considerations—after the production and marketing itself—is the issue of credit. If you can grow and dry acres of flowers and herbs, and find customers for them, you will be asked to give them credit. They want your material, and they think they can sell it to their retail customers. But they need some time to pay you for it as they have product coming in from many sources every day. They have to keep a large stock on hand to satisfy their customers, etc. You will be pushed almost immediately into the question of giving credit to your customers. The country runs on credit, shouldn't you give it, too?

From my own experience in the garment business several years ago, I can tell you that this credit question can become the bane of any small business owner, if he or she doesn't take it seriously right from the beginning. Your first emphasis will be on sales, with the belief that everything will turn out all right if you can just sell enough stuff. That's only partially true. You will probably be OK **if** you can both sell enough and **get paid for it.**

Most small businesses can (and will), all too easily, get caught in a "credit crunch" because, as a beginning business, almost no one will want to give **you** credit for the purchases needed to run your business. You're too new, have no proven track record, and so forth. Yet you will be expected to give credit to all of those already **in** business who want to sell your product. Only a short time of operating like this with your own money going out the front door for your own needs, and only delayed money (30, 60, 90 days and more after shipping) coming in the back door, can leave all but the most well financed new business right up against the wall begging their own bankers for mercy. Trust me. I know. I've been there. It's called the cash flow problem and it is **the** big problem for most small, under-financed businesses, whether you are selling dried thyme or fresh echinacea root, handmade soap, or books about herbs.

If you give a lot of credit, then when this country goes through one of its frequent "downturns in the business cycle," the first people to get hurt financially will no doubt be the newer, smaller shops—the ones you've sold all of your dried flower bunches to. Chances are they will have sold at least half your product when they go bankrupt and you will get in a long line (after the landlords and utility companies and the major suppliers) waiting for your money. We both know you have better things to do with your time—and money.

So what's the answer? Don't sell to little shops? That may be where all your business is. Demand cash on delivery? COD can turn off a lot of sales, too.

A far better system is the one Eric Brandt-Meyer has recently chosen after suffering himself from the painful lesson of giving too-easy credit. He has now discontinued offering new "Net 30 days" accounts. That means he has quit offering to ship goods accompanied by an invoice asking for the net (not discounted)

Good Earth Farm, Freeport, Maine

payment in 30 days. He does continue to offer those more liberal terms to his older, reliable accounts, but he has recently switched to a system of offering only MasterCard® or Visa® as credit terms to new accounts. His bank set him up with the new system and now he can take any order on the telephone or by mail or fax and then, by telephone and modem through his computer system, he can get an authorization number for his "charge account" orders. He can sell to anyone with a valid charge card. Most people in business have a personal charge card, if not a business card. They will protect their own personal credit by keeping up those payments. If a customer gives Eric a number that doesn't "authorize," he simply calls the customer and tells him he'll have to ship COD for this order.

I think this system is really a boon for small businesses and I would urge anyone considering giving credit on their billing to look first at getting into the MasterCard/Visa system. These are operated through your local bank. If you have a good relationship there, you shouldn't have any trouble getting their cooperation. You will need to give them some estimates about how much business you think you will be doing, so that they can see if yours will be a worthwhile account. Our own experience is that whatever estimate you make, chances are the system will get even more use than that. Then, every week, you will be sent a booklet of no longer authorized account numbers. Additionally, you must get an authorization number from the MasterCard/Visa System to charge anything over a certain limit—usually $50. The paperwork is relatively simple, the fees to start and continue in the system are fairly reasonable. These systems help you keep dealing with reputable accounts, and keep you away from unreliable accounts. It offers a very easy way to give some credit to accounts you don't know and to keep your goods moving into the market. After you have dealt with an account for awhile, you may want to offer them some credit, but great caution is necessary.

One big problem to overcome in this whole beginning wholesale routine is that feeling you will have of seeming like a wimp and an amateur if you can't play ball like the big guys do. *Everyone gives us credit. Just ask around. Of course we are good for it. We've been in business for years.* It all sounds so reassuring. Plug thy ears. Smile, and repeat after me: *Boy, I'd really like to give credit, but we are so new that my banker would kill me if I do that. I can take MasterCard® or Visa®, half pre-payment or full COD. I just can't give credit my first year or so in business.*

Meanwhile, back at the farm, Eric finds his new customers by attending the Gift Shows on the east coast a few times a year, and then keeping in touch with those customers by mailers and by phone during the rest of the year to see what they need. These gift shows are huge marketing events held in several major centers around the country where wholesale and retail people are brought together for a few days of intense commercial endeavor. Believe me, these are big events for everyone from the smallest shop owner to buyers for the largest chain stores, and for makers and growers and producers of everything from dried flowers to crystal paperweights, notepaper to occasional tables, prose and poetry books to decorative mirrors—anything anyone might consider a "gift."

One of the best ways to find out about this entire wholesale selling process in America is to talk a shop owner friend into taking you along to the next gift show in your area. You will see in a hurry if this is something you want to be a part of. Besides, you might have a lot of fun and learn more than any book can ever teach you about what small businesses (and large) are all about in this country. I have been both buyer and seller at these shows. They are exhausting and crazy and yes, fun, in a weird sort of revealing way. This is what a lot of America (and much of the western world) is all about. Why not take a close-up look and see if it ought to be part of your world?

Eric doesn't have any "reps" in the field—salespeople who travel around different areas of the country from shop to shop selling a line of products they represent. These people work on commissions, and often represent several compatible products that they believe will sell to the same types of shop. Eric says he hasn't needed such sales help yet, and hasn't been willing to deal with the added problems they might bring. "Reps" aren't employees in the ordinary sense of the word, but they can give you that same feeling and sense of responsibility towards them. They are out there working for you. That makes them and their problems a part of your life.

He does have employees on the farm. Twelve or 15 at a very busy time, six or seven when things slow down. Freeport, Maine, is the site of a huge outlet mall, the '90s version of America's love affair with shopping malls. There are over a hundred discount stores surrounding the world famous mail order giant, L. L. Bean: their store and headquarters. This shopping carnival is now a destination spot for thousands and thousands of travelers every day with large lots for recreational vehicle parking and restaurants and motels springing up all around. Good Earth Farm must compete with all of these outlets for employees, as farm wages are seldom much higher than retail wages.

Brandt-Meyer depends on people who love to work outside. On people who love plants and flowers. I hear this often from small growers: they do best with people who love plants, who find growing things almost therapeutic, who love to be outdoors.

Eric is careful not to hire people who would be counting on the job so much that they might lose their home if his own business suffers from a whole season of bad weather. He hires lots of teenagers and even more Moms, who often need flexible schedules in order to meet family needs. "I can work around those needs," he says, "and they can work around mine."

These women put the dried flowers into bunches, wrap them and ship them in large brown cardboard cartons that Eric got from a shoe company in Freeport. "They didn't need this size, and it has already saved me $5,000 to use them." He also uses newspapers for the top packing material in the cartons, and encloses an employee signed card to guarantee and personalize the shipment, and to explain their efforts at recycling.

Eric says he often imagines beautiful new white boxes with *The Good Earth Farm* emblazoned on them, and white tissue paper packing that he's certain would impress their customers and appear more professional. But the budget, and the chance to recycle, always win out. He'd have to raise his prices to cover the costs, and he'd end up feeling guilty about using all that bleached paper product. This is another pattern we found in visiting many small growers and business people: the young business people in this country are making a commitment to recycling early on in their efforts, and then staying with it.

When he has "certain employees who are very good at it," Eric will often sell more elaborate bouquets of dried flowers. He still does one major craft show every year with other organic growers in Maine. He sells a lot of retail product at that fair and even gets some new wholesale customers, besides touching base again with the whole network of herb and flower people in the area.

He starts his herbs and flowers in a large greenhouse beside the barn. Eric grows on more leased land than his own five acres and grows Christmas trees on the side. He also buys some flower product from other growers in order to ship a more complete line of dried flowers and herbs. Ann still works part-time off the farm.

They have held on to one very successful practice learned in their vegetable growing days: the Fall Pumpkin Hayrides that have just begun at the time of our visit, and will continue for the next few weeks. Families and school children come out every day, seven days a week between 9 AM and 5 PM to ride out into the fields and pick out a big pumpkin to take home. They also get a tiny, free pumpkin and a glass of cider for the $3 the ride costs. In the next few weeks after our visit, several thousand people will visit the Good Earth Farm, and pay that small fee for the privilege of spending a little time at a working farm and getting in touch with that rural feeling we still seem to have buried within us.

Selling Herbs in Pots

ONE VERY EASY way to sell herbs is when they are growing in two or three inch pots which the customer can take home to either plant in the garden or put on a kitchen windowsill. They can either be started by seeds directly in the pots or in seed trays and then transplanted to the pots after the first real leaves appear.

Many herb farms start out with someone just selling pots of herbs and the business grows on from there. In Walpole, New Hampshire, we stopped at the home of Lois Kenyon who for four years has opened her backyard to locals and visitors where she sells potted herbs in a tiny little backyard nursery.

Last year the local garden center took some of her herbs to sell, and the local chamber of commerce listed her herb business on a touring guide. Now tour buses are beginning to stop by full of travelers who want to walk through her fine garden and purchase a few herbs to take home.

Recently, some friends and neighbors helped her put in a little nature trail through her three acres, and she now charges a dollar for visitors to her garden. Not a big business by any means, but something she can handle on her own (Lois was recently widowed) with the little herb business adding to her income.

I have sold potted herbs at farmers' markets, and at local garden centers. During the spring, when everyone seems willing to buy plants, other stores, like the neighborhood hardware stores, also get into the herb plant business. I have sold plants to them, too. But come with me to a fully fledged potted herb grower in Georgia, where we can learn some details of the joys and pitfalls to be found in potting up your herbs.

Sally Barksdale—Georgia

Many herb growers begin their growing careers just as Sally Barksdale did. She wanted some herbs, couldn't find what she wanted, and so started them herself in the backyard. One thing led to another, and now Sally owns and operates a fairly large small business, growing potted herbs for the central Georgia area. We visited during the winter of her sixth year of operation and found that she is now moving into supplying other types of perennial plants, although herbs are still a large part of her business—probably a $50,000 portion for the growing year of our visit. Learning about some of the choices she had to make between those first tiny steps and where her business is now made our visit seem worthwhile.

Barksdale grew up in a gardening family, studied horticulture at the Abraham Baldwin Agricultural College and couldn't wait to get her hands off the books and back into the dirt. She then went to work doing landscape installations. It was during this period that she began growing her first herbs, found that she could grow lots more than she needed, and started supplying neighbors and friends with pots of herbs.

She calls her business Thyme after Thyme, and has a pretty little Herbs for Sale sign in front of her old fashioned small clapboard house which sits on five acres and fronts Athens Road in the little town of Winterville. She still does a nice retail business here but, almost from the beginning, Sally chose to be a wholesale supplier of potted herbs to garden centers in the Atlanta area, about 75 miles away. Herbs were fairly new in the area then, and she sensed she could tie up a part of that market, if she made the effort. Her very first wholesale venture was to simply put her extra herbs in the back of her pickup truck and go down the highway looking for customers. The customers were definitely there. She needed to grow more herbs.

First she built what she calls her cloches: very low, long, plas-
tic-over-pvc pipe tunnels, where she could protect her plants
during what can be the severe temperature drops of Georgia win-
ters. The cloches have an irrigation line on top with a ball-valve
misting system inside each cloche. They were inexpensive to
build, and can be opened from the non-windy side by simply
folding the plastic back. She covered her gallon pot areas with
plastic tarps in the winter. She uses gallon jugs filled with sand
to hold her plastic down as "rocks just tear up everything." Over
the years Sally has been replacing these simple systems with
greenhouses—she now has 12—but only two are heated, and
then only when the temperature drops below 25°.

Sally is still quite young, with an attractive, low-voiced, self-
deprecating manner that doesn't quite cover up the fierce determination that has allowed her to get this far with such a
successful operation. What was it like, I wondered, to grow so
fast and learn all the business and horticultural practices at the
same time? She made some big mistakes, she readily admits.
Like giving credit to her first accounts.

"I'd run out to the mailbox every day," she recalls, "expecting
those checks to be in there. Then it got to be so much, that I
thought for sure that UPS would have to bring it. They simply
couldn't send that much money through the mail. But that didn't
happen either. It's hard to be a bank," she says, "when you're first
starting out."

Now she has gone to a cash sale with almost everyone except
for the largest chains she sells to. "COD is where it's at," she
advises any newcomers to the business world. "Every little business that you give credit to can go out of business so easily in the
next recession and you won't get paid. Period." Sally also doesn't
accept credit cards in her wholesale or retail business. For her,
cash is what business is about. Her retail business still accounts
for about 30 percent of her yearly income.

At first she tried mixing her own soil for the pots, but Georgia soil is thick, red, beautiful and, according to Sally, a total di-
saster for potting because it simply won't drain. She soon came

to realize she was spending too much time at those attempts at mixing and not getting good, consistent results. At the size her business is now, mixing her own soil would also mean getting a tractor, keeping it in repair and building a storage area for it.

She figures soil, which now comes delivered in 25 to 60 yard lots, costs her about a nickel for a 3½"x3½" plastic pot. She and her employees load the six-pack of pots with one pass of the shovel in a little work area behind the house. Every plant gets a pre-printed tag. She charges 75 cents to a dollar wholesale for that pot, once it's filled with growing herbs.

She orders her pots in large quantities a couple of times a year, and has come to use the 3½ inch size after trying other, larger sizes that simply weren't cost effective: they took too long to fill up, took up too much space in the holding areas.

In the beginning, she sold only what she could plant or germinate herself. Now, like many other small growers, she buys some pre-germinated plants and quite a bit of bare root material (lavenders, horseradish, raspberries) that she can simply pot up and allow to grow on.

She suggests that new people, trying to start such a business, begin only with what they can do themselves, learn the best seed companies to deal with and, through them, learn the best suppliers for such additional material. The more exotic the herb you want to grow, she says, the smaller will be the seed house to supply it.

She sells herbs by the tray, nine of each variety, eighteen to the tray. In the spring she does tray assortments for new and smaller accounts. She sells primarily to nurseries and garden centers, hardware stores and, recently, to some health food stores. Her primary selling is done by routes she has established. She or an employee will cover that route on a particular day, delivering the orders, always watching for potential new accounts along the route, and always following a rule she established from the beginning: never drive by a potential account without stopping— at least twice.

She asked for minimums in the early days, but soon gave that up. "You never know when some tiny little customer is going to grow up into a very big and best customer. I treat everyone the same and, by having routes, we can easily drop off even small re-orders without a lot of cost." Starting in July, "when the spring madness is completely over," she will load up the truck with beautiful plants and go out selling from then until October. She moves a lot of plants that way, she says, filling in and replacing for her customers.

Barksdale gets totally frustrated by the lack of care her plants will sometimes get after she delivers them, and she often offers some help to the retailers because of that. The overhead water-ing systems that many nurseries install are her particular enemy. "They simply don't do a good job." If her plants need water at the nurseries she sells to she will usually tell an employee about that, but if the whole herb section is a mess she will often take time to straighten it out and make the plants look much more saleable. She learns a lot, she says, by making many of these de-liveries herself. It gives her a chance to check out the competi-tion, to see what is really selling, and to help her in her choices as she starts moving more and more into perennials.

Her truck is an Isuzu Cube Van which she purchased only a year ago and which (because of its carrying capacity of 300 trays) caused her to get out and sell a lot more. "We had our biggest spurt of growth ever this last year," she says, "and, frankly, it was just too much. I want to slow down a bit this next year and ab-sorb the reality of all this growth, and take a little breathing space. My sister also came to help this past season and that, and the new truck, allowed me to go all out with the sales. I need some time now to reassess and think about the future."

The University of Georgia is close by in Athens. It has a very strong horticulture department and Sally can get help there in many ways. Most of her employees work part-time with the plants, between classes and exams. She can also go there to at-tend seminars and to continue her own education in horticulture. If she has a plant pest or disease problem, she can go over there and get assistance. The University also offers her new varieties to try growing.

Like other growers, she is quite frustrated at not being able to pay good employees what they are worth. So far, there's just not enough profit to do that. She has six part-time people during the winter, and up to 10 or 12 people beginning early in the year. She has a little time clock on the back porch of her home. She would like to hire more elderly people because of their strong love and knowledge of plants, but the work is hard physically and "the speed everyone has to move" means only the young and very physically able can keep up with the pace.

Her sales routes are starting to change now as Atlanta, like many large cities, becomes far too competitive and a "dumping ground for discounters." She is working on establishing new routes out towards Spartanburg, in South Carolina. Herbs, she says, are becoming good sellers everywhere, not just in big cities.

She is also trying hard to decide not to let her company grow any bigger. Sally is still a very young woman—she started the business in her early twenties—with a remarkably successful business that is completely debt free. She's never even wanted to borrow any money for the business, because "then all you're doing is working for the bank." But the costs to her, personally, must have been enormous. There is an undertone of loss in her voice that makes her admonitions to new growers especially strong. Listen carefully to Sally Barksdale, if you're thinking about starting a potted herb business.

"You know, I really didn't think about all this at the beginning," she says, with a wave of her arm at the "all this" that she has built up from a few pots of herbs in her back yard. "At that point I could only think about a half hour ahead of time, and where I needed to be. No foresight whatsoever. I was having fun. I was growing flowers. I had no idea about the commitment I was making. I had no idea that I'd never be able to take a vacation. I was just so happy to find something I love to do. That's typical, I guess, of people in their early twenties. You're absorbed with starting your own business, and then suddenly, the years have gone by and you notice you're worn out. What happened, you ask yourself?

"I talk to other self-employed people and they have the same problem. This one is very, very labor intensive so that you always feel you have to get back out there and do something else. This has been like getting married and adopting a billion children. The plants need so much care. They really are such a commitment."

And under it all, there is still such a love of working with plants in the dirt—something she has less and less time for. She is at an in-between stage right now and going back and forth in her mind about whether to get bigger or smaller. Planning to get into more varieties, planning to cut back in sales—almost in the same breath.

"I feel like I'm at a bottleneck," says Sally. "You get to be management instead of a grower. It's a real Catch 22. You're too small to hire the right people, too big not to." She's in stop and start, forward and reverse, trying to work it out and make the next decision be the right one for her. If I had to guess which way she'd go, I'd only guess one thing: that she would make a success out of whatever she chose to do—and probably worry every step of the way.

Ernest Pugh and Ron Engeland Grow Garlic, Washington State

"I'VE GOT A little extra land. I want to grow some herbs that will make me some money. What should I grow?" I get these calls quite often, usually from people who have heard of expensive medicinal herbs and want me to tell them which ones of those exotic herbs to grow.

Growing medicinal herbs would only make sense if you already knew the medicine makers who would buy your crop. There are no central or large regional markets for medicinal herbs around the country, like the vegetable, or even the culinary herb markets, with price lists and lots of interested customers. Yes, some people do find markets for medicinal herbs, and the other chapters on herbal products and wildcrafting will cover some of that information, and give you some ideas about where to look for such markets. So will the reference sections. I also think that before long there will be more markets for small medicinal growers as the naturopathic schools around the country graduate more doctors, and as the demand for organically grown medicinal herbs increases.

Meanwhile, I often suggest that new or would-be small commercial growers give some serious thought to organically grown garlic as a crop on small acreage, because it is one of the world's most beneficial plants, it is becoming more popular every year, and because most people don't seem to realize what wonderful varieties of garlic are out there waiting to be grown and introduced in your area.

Good garlic is also relatively easy to grow, easy to sell at a decent price and it can be turned into art work—braids and wreaths which can be sold at very, very good prices. There are still more interesting things about garlic growing that might encourage you to consider such a crop.

Allium sativum ophioscordon, "ophio" garlic

The garlic market is dominated by what is commonly called California garlic: the papery white, long-storing, sometimes hot tasting, everyday garlic most readers probably have in their kitchens at this very moment. Your supply no doubt came from an area just south of San Francisco, where up to 90 per cent of the garlic grown and processed in the U.S. comes from. The little town of Gilroy, California, is the center of that garlic universe. Hundreds of thousands of people attend their now famous annual garlic festivals, and an estimated hundred million pounds of garlic are grown, processed and distributed through Gilroy each year. This very big American garlic source is even now being challenged by enormous shipments of very cheap garlic imports from China.

Am I recommending you jump into competition with all of that? On maybe a half acre of ground? Certainly not. What I am suggesting is that you learn a little bit about the other 10 per cent of the garlic growing world that exists in this country, and that may hold the key to a successful crop for you.

I am grateful to two sources for most of this information on garlic. One is the recent and delightful book (see page 69) by Ron L. Engeland of Filaree Farms in the eastern part of my own state of Washington, and the other is Ernest Pugh, a local producer on our own island who has grown garlic here for 15 years and has worked out many of the problems that can so frustrate new garlic growers.

Engeland's book sets out the central premise very well: that there are two basic types of garlic grown in this country, but that only one type, the softneck *Allium sativum sativum* is seriously grown and marketed in the country, primarily because of its long storage life. The other type, *Allium sativum ophioscordon*, has a much shorter storage life but a much finer flavor, with cloves that are more easily peeled than those of the softnecks. The softneck garlics have thickish leaves, vaguely resembling those of Dutch Iris, and no flower stem. The "ophio" garlics have lovely coiled flower stalks that shoot up in the spring, make a graceful circular curve and then produce tiny, flavorful flower blossoms. These stalks are usually, though not always, cut off in commercial garlic production, and home gardeners like myself often leave them on for the tasty blossoms and the splendid bouquet additions of the flower stalks.

Under these two basic types of garlic, there are five basic varieties, with the Rocambole variety of the ophios considered the most flavorful and delicious by almost everyone who discovers and tastes them. Unfortunately, the Rocamboles are rather short lived, usually lasting after harvest only through November or December. Come late winter or spring and we're almost all using the Gilroy garlics and darned glad to have them.

Much of the beginning of Engeland's fascinating book is devoted to this attempt to clarify the types of garlic available, plus some very interesting geographical and historical perspectives about garlic, but the bulk of the book is his detailed instructions and hints to garlic growers everywhere. His farm is in north central Washington state on the far (as in cold) side of the Cascade range, not too far from the Canadian border.

I live on the west side of those mountains and get my instructions on garlic growing from my friend Ernest Pugh, who grows in this maritime range of the Pacific Northwest.

Like Engeland, Ernest used to plant his garlic in the fall, "aiming for All Saints Day and trying to get it all in by the second week of November, before any severe weather." But in this area that is still harvest time and often the busiest time for any growers.

One year Ernest just couldn't make his end-of-October planting date and ended up having to plant in January. He was relieved and surprised to find that his January-planted garlic was full-sized and fully mature by fair time, the third week in August. Furthermore, the January planting precludes a problem we sometimes have here: a warm spell in mid-winter that stimulates too much early growth, followed by hard freezing that can do some crop damage. So Ernest has planted in January ever since, and now produces about 1500 heads of garlic, in three varieties, each year.

Engeland plants in the fall and produces many, many thousands of heads a year in over 300 different strains. Garlic, both Engeland and Pugh believe, is a highly adaptable plant that can probably be grown everywhere in the United States and one that is also highly saleable almost everywhere. The key to the sales is in growing premium quality garlic, and in being one of the first growers in your area to do so.

Ernest's property lies close to our community sand and gravel pit—"great glaciated sand particles" he calls the soil there. The drainage is magnificent, but he has to dig a two-foot-wide hole just to set a fence post.

Pugh agrees with Engeland, who claims that small commercial garlic growers need to realize that "soil preparation is often the deciding factor that determines success or failure" in producing choice garlic.

Over the last 15 years, Pugh has managed to build up an absolutely lush foot of velvety, chocolate-colored, first class tilth

Ernest Pugh's Fertilizer Recipe

Fishmeal	**4 pints**
Rock Phosphate	**2 pints**
Kelp Meal	**1 pint**
Dolomitic Lime	**1/2 pint**

This is enough for his 1500 plants; keep the same ratios to increase or decrease the amount.

that carries his extensive gardens and the garlic: He does sheet composting—"because that's the most efficient system, and you don't end up with piles of muck"—with both his garden and kitchen waste, plus sheep manure from certain island farmers who don't use what he calls "the bad stuff"—feed that is full of hormones and antibiotics.

The garden beds are so fluffy that he uses half inch plywood, 12 inches wide and eight feet long for paths into the garden. Remarkably, he has no slug problems (the bane of all northwest gardeners) because his "property is not close to the woods, it is dry, and quite alkaline." The beds are also immaculate.and tended daily. "I think I only found three slugs this year," says Ernest.

He hand digs the garlic beds each year, with occasional help from a tiny rototiller. Before planting, he puts in a fertilizer mixture at the root zone of the garlic.

That is the basic food for the garlic, except for a very occasional addition of manure tea, made from the sheep manure, cut in half with water, to which he adds a half pound of blood meal for each fifty gallon drum. He uses this liquid feed primarily for his brassicas, perhaps only once or twice a season on the garlic.

In 15 years of growing garlic, neither Pugh nor Engeland has ever had any disease problems. Never. Any. Garlic disease problems are fairly common and can be truly horrendous, especially in high rainfall areas such as the Pacific Northwest—although I must add that these particular islands in Puget Sound are well-known for their lack of rainfall in the summer. Almost every season I hear of at least one regional garlic grower who has a crop failure, so Ernest's good luck is quite worth talking about. You can read about these garlic disease problems in Engeland's book, but meanwhile, both men credit several things for their untainted record with this crop, the first of which is an absolutely, positively, never-fail system of three-year crop rotation. I visited Ernest's place again today, while he was planting garlic. He will not plant a single clove of garlic in that section again for three years.

After preparing the ground, Ernest usually lays six sheets of newspaper over each bed, to begin his effort to keep weeding, one of the most important yet tedious jobs required in growing garlic, to an absolute minimum. He then wets the newspaper to prepare for planting. This year, instead of the newspaper, he was trying a roll of 36" kraft building paper (the cost is 8¢ per foot from the local lumber company) as the day was windy and the newspapers often blow away.

He usually plants the garlic on a six inch triangular grid using a tool he has fabricated for the job. Very careful garlic planting is another of those important, yet repetitious jobs that are necessary for great garlic. Ernest's metal-working skills have made this tedious job a lot easier. The steel pipe planter stands about three and a half feet tall, is about 13 inches wide and 28 inches long, with punch points of about three inch lengths. It takes two people to operate it easily. They step once lightly on the bar of the planter and it makes 25 planting holes two to three inches deep; they move forward a step or two, put the back row of metal punches in the prints of the forward holes they just made, and make 17 new holes; then move forward making 17 holes with each step on the planter. It is a splendid system, easy on the back and uniform as can be. Ernest intends to make a new planter soon, out of lightweight aluminum that he can operate by himself, but this one has served him very well over the years.

Today he shows me an alternative method that anyone can use to achieve the same results. He cut out a 30-inch square plywood board, and then placed holes (with a 1¼" hole saw) on a six-inch triangular grid pattern (four holes in one line, five in the next) to lay on the soft soil. He placed a piece of bright tape a little less than three inches from the sharpened bottom of a broom handle and quickly punched in the triangular pattern of planting holes. The kraft paper fits nicely under the board and with his plywood planks through the garden he can easily walk along and plant the cloves quickly—being careful, of course, to get each clove with its root side down. He then goes along the rows with a little bucket full of purchased planting mix—"Uncle Malcolm's potting soil from Canada is my favorite these days, probably because of that ridiculous name"—and drops in half a handful to cover the clove.

After planting, he puts a full foot of oat/wheat straw mulch over the beds, which will settle down by spring to four or five inches, just enough, he says, to keep the weeds at bay. "The mulch keeps the soil bugs up near the surface," says Ernest, "which is where they belong, making that beautiful tilth." The garlic pops up through the mulch in such a regular pattern that, whenever there are blank spaces, he can peek under to locate any problems. The most common problem is to find an occasional garlic taking off under the newspaper instead of up through the mulch. A little tug with the crook of his finger on the new green shoot usually sets it straight.

Ernest grows three basic types of garlic every year, primarily to make his supply last until the following harvest. The Rocamboles are his favorite ("I can, and often do, eat them like grapes") but they don't last too long. The other two varieties, Italian Red and Silver Skin, are longer lasting but have a little less flavor. He also tries out a few new varieties each year to keep bringing in new stock and tasting new flavors. "If you ate noth-

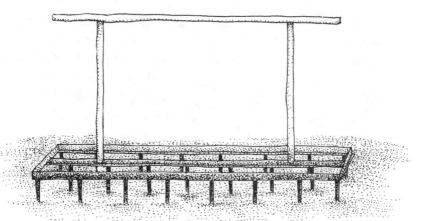

Ernest Pugh's garlic planter

ing but supermarket tomatoes," he tells me, "and judged every
tomato on that basis, you would simply quit eating tomatoes. So
let's keep up the varieties."

Ernest put in sprinklers a few years ago. If he had it to do
over again now, he says, he'd probably put in a soaker hose system which would mean re-doing all the garden configurations.
The cost of island water is going up this month, to become the
most expensive in the state. The island is growing too fast, and
the water supply is less than expected. Ernest and every other
gardener on the island must look hard now at everything concerning water. We're growling at a small town government that
has managed to pass out permits for unlimited development including breweries, car washes, and auto-body shops, while begging all the residents to conserve. But we all realize this is going
on everywhere, and that water and water quality are fast bub-
bling up as the big issues, not just for the '90s, but for the coming century. Anyone contemplating even a small garlic venture,
or any other small agricultural endeavor, must consider the water question as one of the primary issues, right along with the
land and the soil.

Ernest cuts the flower stalks off the ophio varieties along
about late May or early June, "before they start to curl." The

Engeland book has an interesting discussion on this issue and concludes (almost) that waiting to remove the flower stalks until they stand up straight and harden off will lead to longer storage life for the bulbs. Engeland says some garlic growers dispute his claim and, at least among ophio growers, this is probably one of those questions that may go on forever, never being quite resolved one way or another.

Ernest harvests towards the end of August, always testing first, of course. He has had only one or two extra cool and rainy summers, when the garlic wasn't ready at that time. Engeland gives more detailed information on harvesting by variety and by the number of green leaves left—usually recommending that five or six green leaves be left above ground. Both say you should not treat garlic as onions, knocking them over before harvest. And that you should decrease the moisture to the bulbs well before harvest, so that you don't pull them up wet. Both also agree about not washing the bulbs after they are harvested. When Ernest pulls up the bulbs and lays them on the ground for a couple of days to begin curing, they still have great juicy leaves on them. In Engeland's region, it is much too hot in late summer to let the garlic lie on the ground, so he takes them into a shed for the first drying.

During these few days of curing, Ernest keeps tarps handy just in case we should get a rainfall. Moisture on the garlic at this point must be avoided. Then he ties them in clusters, 12 or 15 plants to the bunch. He uses binder twine and a clove hitch near the top of the greens. He ties two of these clusters with a four foot piece of twine and puts them over a rafter in the woodshed where there is air circulating all the time, and no chance for dampening. He leaves them hanging like that for a couple of months.

Just before our real winter weather begins, Ernest takes the garlic down from the woodshed rafter, cuts off the now dried leaves, leaving a two inch stem. He then places them in netted bags in his "chill rooms" where the humidity is low, the temperature is about 36° to 42° and where outdoor air is circulated in by fans. Whatever you do, he warns, "keep them out of heavy, stagnant moist air, which is really the amniotic fluid for bacteria."

In December, Ernest does the other very important job that has protected his garlic from disease over the years. "I am a maniac about grading for seed stock," he says. He divides the bulbs in December and carefully examines every bulb and puts them into three classes. Number one best quality is for seed. Never a dot of pink or brown on them, he says, never a tiny speck of mold. These individual cloves are set aside for January planting. These are not whole bulbs but individual cloves, "often only one clove, but always the healthiest clove from a bunch." Number two best quality is to store, still in the nets, still in the chill rooms. Number three quality is to use as soon as possible.

All this effort to get perfect garlic is done so that I and other island residents may enjoy the delicious food at the little bakery and restaurant Ann Di Giovanni runs on the property she shares with Ernest. The Isis bakery is a favorite, almost hidden island spot that reminds us all of the reasons we first moved to the island, the *echt* that remains in this fast changing environment. He has done garlic braids and wreaths in the past, but the little restaurant and their own love of garlic now use up this garlic supply quite easily. Ernest also grows almost all the other vegetables for the restaurant.

The Engeland book has a garlic marketing chapter in it. But the cultivation chapters are the most important ones, because good money can only be made on **great** garlic; gourmet garlic, if you will, that is definitely different in look and taste from the ordinary garlic available in most places, most of the time. If you take real care, you can get a product that large farmers simply cannot produce because it requires so much hand labor. And the level to start at, I think, is the level I've described here—small quantities, for premium quality. I also think that I can guarantee that you won't have any trouble selling that kind of garlic. Seed stock is available from Engeland's farm and from several seed houses around the country, a few of which are listed in the reference section following these chapters.

References For Herb Growing

EACH SECTION IN this book is followed by a reference section to help lead you into ever more information about your particular interest in herbs. This first section also includes much general resource information on herbs, especially about the publications and associations that make up the primary herbal business network around the country. I would also recommend that the reader find the time to read each reference section throughout the book as there is important cross-over information.

HERB PUBLICATIONS

The Business of Herbs. Published bimonthly by Northwind Farm Publications. 1 yr. subscription is $20 from Rt. 2 Box 246, Shevlin, MN 56676-9535.

This is the first key to entering the commercial herb network in the country. The editors and publishers, Paula and David Oliver, cover the field—from plant profiles to soap making, from the latest machinations of the FDA to the future possibilities in aromatherapy. Even the ads are helpful, and so are the book reviews, calendar of Herb Happenings, and science and business notes. If you can only afford one herb business publication, start with this one. It will lead you in towards everything else. They also publish an Herb Resource Directory, with informative paragraphs about herb businesses around the country.

HerbalGram, Published quarterly by the American Botanical Council and the Herb Research Foundation. $25 per year from PO Box 201660, Austin, Texas 78720. 512-331-8868. FAX 512-331-1924.

Here is the journal of choice for those whose primary interests are in the herb plants themselves, their chemical properties, and the world-wide studies on herbs. If you should wonder if herbs might be just a trendy fad that will soon pass, I recommend a subscription to HerbalGram. In fact, I recommend it to anyone with a serious interest in herbs, and especially in herbal medicine.

There are also reports in each issue on what the media have been reporting on herbs, a market report for world-wide availability and pricing on herbs, book reviews, and calendar, plus feature articles ranging from bio-diversity to AIDS research, from complete plant profiles to tiny bits of interesting news about about all things herbal.

The Herb Companion, published bimonthly by Interweave Press, Inc. Subscription is $21 per year from 306 North Washington Ave., Loveland, CO 80537. 303-669-7672.

Connects the herb-working world to the rest of the herb-interested population. A well done consumer journal with primary accents on the culinary, crafts, decorative, and garden aspects, rather than on medicinal herbs. Complete reviews of herbal and garden books. Recipes, interesting ads, columns and articles by well known herbalists.

The Herbal Connection, published bimonthly by the Herb Growing & Marketing Network. Available for $24 per year from PO Box 245, Silver Spring, PA 17575-0245. 717-3903-3295.

The newsletter is very business oriented. The editor, Maureen Rogers, is a CPA with a strong business bent and interest in helping small business herb people deal with realities—especially concerning costs and financing, insurance, publicity, etc. Many articles in the newsletter are reprints from a variety of sources that she monitors. She also publishes the Herbal Green Pages, an excellent directory, published every two years, with alphabetical listings of nearly 2,000 herbal businesses. Your business can be listed in the Green Pages free of charge. Cost for the directory is $20 postpaid.

Herb Quarterly, PO Box 689, San Anselmo, CA 94960. 415-455-9540. FAX 415 455-9541. $24 year.

The offices of this magazine seem to move around the country with great regularity, but the articles and drawings remain fairly constant: friendly, inviting, and strong on recipes, gardening and crafts, along with herbal medicine tradition and folklore.

HERB ASSOCIATIONS

International Herb Growers and Marketers Association, Known as IHGMA. 1202 Allanson Rd., Mundelein, IL 60060. 708-949-4372.

The primary commercial herb association in the country. Membership rates vary depending on the size of your business. The association sponsors the only large herbal business get-together each year, with regional seminars in between. If you are serious about an herbal business, you should definitely consider joining this association whose purpose is to promote the production, marketing, and use of herbs and herb related products through education and research. A friendly, welcoming network. They now offer a mentor program for new members.

American Herb Association, PO Box 1673, Nevada City, CA 95959. Regular membership is $20 per year. Director and editor is Kathi Keville.

An educational and research organization with a quarterly newsletter. Strongest focus is on medicinal herbs, rather than culinary or decorative uses. Good source of international herbal news, herb book reviews, herb seminars, classifieds, etc.

Herb Research Foundation, 1007 Pearl St., Ste 200, Boulder, CO 80302. 303-449-2265. FAX 303-449-7849.

Co-publishers of HerbalGram (see above), and leaders in the effort to strengthen the scientific basis of American herbalism. The foundation provides accurate and reliable information on botanicals and does research on herbs. Working now on a Botanical Ingredients Review for medicinal plants and the translations into English of botanical monographs used in Germany for approval there of herbal products. Membership is $35.

American Herbalists Guild, PO Box 1683, Soquel, CA 95073.

The professional organization for medical herbalists, they provide referrals and work to promote ever better education and training for herbalists.

See the **Reference Section on Herb Farms** for state and regional herb associations.

OTHER PUBLICATIONS WORTH CONSIDERING

Growing for Market, a monthly publication of Fairplain Publications. $26 per year from PO Box 3747, Lawrence, Kansas 66046. Tel. 913 841-2559.

A newsletter for small, primarily organic growers of all produce including herbs and flowers. Gives wholesale produce prices (including herbs), and profiles of growers around the country, book reviews, and reports on agricultural news of interest to market gardeners from around the world. Excellent feature articles on subjects such as hiring interns or apprentices, and how to do a better job at your farmers' market. Realistic. Helpful. Informative.

HortIdeas, A monthly publication from Greg & Pat Williams, 460 Black Lick Road, Gravel Switch, KY 40328. $15 year.

The true gleaners of the horticulture world, they pick up and pass along horticulture information from world-wide sources. From Africanized honey bees to information on xeriscaping—even when their coverage is not relevant to what I'm interested in at the moment, it is so wide reaching and interesting that I save the issues and reread them now and then with renewed interest.

Rural Enterprise, quarterly from PO Box 878, Menomonee Falls, WI 53052. $8.95 yr.

Covers on-farm marketing, farmers' market operations, agricultural diversification, and rural home-based businesses. Strong on sustainable agriculture, organic methods and detailed information to help small growing enterprises grow.

Organic Farmer, a quarterly publication from the Rural Education Action Project. $15 year from 15 Barre St., Montpelier, VT 05602-3504. 802-223-7222. FAX 802-223-0269.

As ideas like sustainable and organic agriculture move into the mainstream, perhaps only magazines like this special one from Vermont can help us keep our heads straight about what all this greening of the country is all about: what's hype and what's real This publication keeps up on the complex effort to institute national standards for organic farming. They also glean from organic newsletters and publications around the country and the world.

Produce News, 2185 Lemoine Ave., Fort Lee, NJ 07024-6088. 201-592-9100. FAX 201-592-0809.

Weekly publication aimed primarily at retail chains and market wholesalers.

Public Market Press. Contact Ted Spitzer, PMP, 5454 Palisade Ave., Bronx, NY 10471. 212-884-5716. (Business of Herbs)

A free newsletter from a nonprofit organization promoting farmers' markets.

Cut Flower Quarterly. Publication of the Association of Specialty Cut Flower Growers, MPO Box 268, Oberlin, OH 44074. 216-774-2887. FAX 216-774-2435.

If cut or dried flowers are a part of your operation, or you want them to be, these are the people with the information you might seek. A friendly, welcoming organization offering a special hand to small growers. Membership dues depend on size.

RECOMMENDED SUPPLIERS

Irrigation

Roberts Irrigation Products, Inc., 700 Rancheros Dr., San Marcos, CA 92069. 619-744-4511. FAX 619-744-0914.

Supplier of thin walled, low-cost, high performance irrigation hose with emission points designed to uniformly irrigate long rows of plants. Contact for dealer near you. (Vegetable Grower.)

Greenhouses

Charley's Greenhouse Supply, 1569 Memorial Highway, Mt. Vernon, WA 98273. 206-428-2626.

They sell greenhouses and a complete line of greenhouse supplies plus other material. Catalog, $2.

Stuppy Greenhouse Mfg., PO Box 12456, North Kansas City, MO 64116. Catalog, free.

Gardener's Supply Co., 128 Intervale Road, Burlington VT 05401.

Greenhouses and a complete line of other supplies. Catalog, free.

Bio-Agriponics, 25935 Detroit Road, Ste. 237, Westlake, OH 44145. 216-835-8662. FAX 216-835-9201.

A new ('94) system aiming to offer greenhouse herb growers tools, equipment and herb marketing assistance. (Business of Herbs)

Plant Tags

Mastertag, 9350 Walsh Road, Montague, MI 49437. 800-253-0439. FAX 800-828-0003.

Sells small and large quantities. Custom message or plain.

Park Seed Wholesale, Cokesbury Road, Greenwood, SC 29647. 800-845-3366.

Pat's "Mini-Pack" Labels, 785 White Road, Watsonville, CA 95076. 408-662-0551.

Sells plain plant markers in smallish quantities, packed with a permanent marking pen.

Beneficial Insects

Gardens Alive, 5100 Schenley Place, Lawrenceburg, IN 47025.

Natural Solutions, Necessary Trading Co., One Nature's Way, New Castle, VA 24127.

DIRECTORIES

Gardening By Mail, by Barbara J. Barton. Published by Houghton Mifflin.

Available at book stores. A wonderful, frequently updated resource for finding plants and other gardening materials and supplies.

Herbs of Commerce. Available from American Botanical Council, PO Box 201660, Austin, TX 78720. $39.50 + $2 postage.

A list of all herb species used in commerce, written to clarify the endless confusion over common names of herbs. Over 550 plants listed, 1800 cross-referenced species.

Sustainable Agriculture Directory of Expertise. Sustainable Agriculture Publications, Hills Bldg, Rm 12, University of Vermont, Burlington, VT 05405.

Lists hundreds of people and groups you can contact for advice on building soil health, broadening your arsenal of pest control tools, diversifying cash flow, and much more. 300 pp. $14.95 ppd.

Herb Companion Wishbook & Resource Guide. 16.95 + p&h from Interweave Press, 201 E. Fourth St., Loveland, CO 80537, publishers of *Herb Companion* Magazine.

Hundreds of mail order sources for all things herbal.

International Directory of Specialists in Herbs, Spices and Medicinal Plants. Available from Dept. of Soil & Plant Sciences, University of Massachusetts, Amherst, MA 01003. $35 plus postage.

List of suppliers of beneficial insects and organisms. Free from Dept. of Pesticide Regulation, Environmental Monitoring and Pest Management Branch, PO Box 942871, Sacramento, CA 94271.

AABGA Internship Directory. $5 from AABGA Internship Directory, 786 Church Rd., Wayne, PA 19087. (Business of Herbs.)

Lists 150 gardens around the USA that have apprenticeship programs for those interested in horticulture.

Ferrel's Jobs in Horticulture. Six issues (3 mo. subscription) $19.95 from 154 E. Chapel Ave., Carlisle, PA 17013-3435. 800-428-2474.

Guide to the U. S. Organic Foods Production Act of 1990. Available for $10 from Stuart Fishman. 503-245-2309.

An explanation "in plain English" of the 1990 act to help growers understand how to obtain organic certification.

Source List for Plants & Seeds, Anderson Horticultural Library. $34.95 from AHL, Minnesota Landscape Arboretum, Box 39, Chanhassen, MN 55317. 612-443-2440.

Recommended source for locating unusual plants and seeds. (Herbal Connection.)

GOVERNMENT RESOURCES

Small Scale Agriculture Office, Department of Agriculture. CSRS; OSSA; Suite 328A, Aerospace Center, Washington, DC 20250-2200. Fax 202-401-1804.

An informative, free newsletter, "Small Scale Agriculture Today," available quarterly. Office is run by Howard "Bud" Kerr, a real enthusiast for small scale agriculture—and for life.

ATTRA NEWS, Quarterly Newsletter of Appropriate Technology Transfer for Rural Areas. PO Box 3657, Fayetteville, AR 72702. Funded by U.S. Fish & Wildlife Service.

ATTRA disseminates information about sustainable agriculture and low-input farming to U.S. farmers, agribusiness, extension agents, wildlife professionals, and other interested people. Their newsletter is free and fascinating as a way to track the revolution taking place in agriculture as it moves into the 21st century and towards a more sustainable future. They publish lots of material on organic certification, cover crops, etc.

Market Reports. U.S. Dept. of Agriculture, AMS, F&V Division, Market News Branch. Room 2503 South Bldg., PO Box 96456, Washington DC 20090-6456.

You can send for a free handbook and subscription prices for market reports. It sounds great, but is not really that useful for small growers dealing in their own area.

Ag Research and Extension Agents

Two key sources for additional information on growing herbs (or almost anything else) are the horticultural and agricultural departments at universities and the state or county extension agents in your area.

In the last century, congress mandated that agricultural research be done at state land-grant universities, and then they created extension services to get that information out into the farm communities. For over a century, this has been a key agricultural program that new, small growers could tap into for help and information.

Unfortunately, these programs, along with so many others, have been drastically cut in recent years and you may or may not still have an extension agent in your area able to offer you information and assistance in growing. To find out, contact your county information officer and ask if there is an agricultural extension service offered in your area. If you still have the service, call or drop in and see the agent to find out just what services are offered. These are experienced people with local knowledge: they know the soil and weather conditions in the area—often they know about marketing and have access to more information than you can imagine. In my area, the county agent is the primary advocate for farming in the county. Sadly, the job is now only part time, and so is much of the farming.

Contact the universities in your state to see about their agriculture/horticulture programs, and to inquire if there are any faculty members with herb or other cash crop or market garden expertise. They can be very helpful.

Master Gardener Program

If your skills at growing aren't what they should be to consider growing herbs commercially, one good place to start improving is with the Master Gardener program. This wonderful program was started in 1972 in Washington state by Extension agents, who were being overwhelmed by the public with home gardening questions. The Master Gardener program started out as a way to train volunteers to help with all those questions. It is also a very serious, very thorough horticultural program of classroom sessions, tours, field days, etc. In our area, it is 60 hours of learning, followed by an exam, followed by volunteer work as pay-back by the student. Many say that the pay-back to the community in volunteer time is even more fun and informative than the classes themselves. The program is now offered in almost every state in the country. You can find out about your closest Master Gardener program by contacting your closest Agriculture Extension agent (see above).

Directory of Master Gardener Programs in the U.S & Canada available from Master Gardeners International Corp., 2904 Cameron Mills Rd., Alexandria, VA 22302. $10 to members, $15 to all others.

Herb Industry Organic Herb Crop Buyers

Frontier Cooperative Herbs. 3021 78th St., Norway, IA 52318. 319-227-7996.

Looking for organically certified herb and spice growers. Write to them for grower guidelines.

Trout Lake Farm, 149 Little Rd., Trout Lake, WA 98650. 509-395-2025. FAX 509-395-2645.

They buy herbs only from **certified** organic growers. Call David Doty for information.

RECOMMENDED CONSULTANTS & INTERNSHIPS

For those with herb growing interests beyond the backyard or very small acreage level, Tom Johnson, of South Dakota, offers consulting services, herb seeds, and entry for new growers into an herb marketing network. For details, contact **TJ Enterprises,** Box 21, Buffalo, SD 57720. 605-375-3504 (Bus. of Herbs)

Alternative agriculture internships are offered by the **Intervale Foundation.** Programs include intern training and support for a community supported agriculture project. Contact Andy Lee, 128 Intervale Rd., Burlington, VT 05401. Lee is author of a popular, respected book on market gardening. See book listings in this section.

Agroecology Program at the University of California. Santa Cruz. 95064. 408-459-2321. Offering six month apprenticeship programs in organic methods in 1994. Contact them to see if program will be continued beyond '94. (HortIdeas).

The January '93 issue of Growing For Market lists the following organizations with programs to link organic farms and apprentices: Northeast Workers on Organic Farms, Box 608, Belchertown, MA 01007; Tilth Apprentice Placement Program, Steve Shelby, Oregon Tilth, 31615 Fern Road, Philomath, OR 97370; Maine Organic Farming and Gardening Assn., Box 2176, Augusta, ME 04338; California Certified Organic Farmers, PO Box 8136, Santa Cruz, CA 95061; Bio-Dynamic Farming and Gardening Assn., PO Box 550, Kimberton, PA 19442.

HERB GROWING BUSINESSES

Elliott Gardens. Bill & Donna Elliott, 6321 Lowell Blvd., Denver, CO 80211

Seabreeze Organic Farm. Stephenie Caughlin, 3909 Arroyo Sorrento Rd., San Diego, CA 92130

Good Earth Farm. Eric & Ann Brandt-Meyer, 55 Pleasant Hill Road, Freeport, ME 04032

Berry Hill Herb Gardens. Lois Kenyon, Box 85, Old Keene Road, Walpole, NH 03608

Thyme After Thyme. Sally Barksdale, 550 Athens Road, Winterville, GA 30683

Isis Bakery. Ernest Pugh, 161 B Dougherty Lane, Friday Harbor, WA 98250

Filaree Farms. Ron Engeland, Rt. 2, Box 162, Okanogan, WA 98840

BOOKS ON GROWING & USING HERBS

I have tried, with few exceptions, to list only books that should be available through your regional library systems. If you decide to purchase books, or you have trouble locating certain books, the following specialized small mail order book companies can be of great help.

MAIL ORDER HERB BOOK SOURCES

American Botanical Council's Bookstore, PO Box 201560, Austin TX 78720.

Ag Access, PO Box 2008, Davis, CA 95617

Capability's Books Inc., 2379 Highway 46, Deer Park, WI 54007

Northwind Farm Publications, Rt. 2, Box 246, Shevlin, MN 56676

Wood Violet Books, 3814 Sunhill Dr., Madison, WI 53704

American Ginseng - Green Gold, by W. Scott Persons. Bright Mountain Books, North Carolina, 1986.

This is the plant that gets all the media coverage because of its high price in the market and its exotic reputation. But theres little reliable information about ginseng easily available. Persons takes a fairly conservative approach (not a lot of wild claims), puts the accent on growing, and writes from the experience of his own ginseng farm in North Carolina.

Backyard Cash Crops, by Craig Wallin. Specialty Crop Digest, Bellingham, WA, 1990.

A great idea book for growing herbs, flowers, and other high value cash crops. Wallin also writes a newsletter on specialty crops and gleans endless information on these crops from many sources. A sample copy of his newsletter is available for $1 to cover postage from Profitable Plants, PO Box 1058, Bellingham, WA 98227.

Backyard Market Gardening: The Entrepreneur's Guide to Selling What You Grow, by Andrew W. Lee. Good Earth Publications, Burlington, VT, 1992.

Growing takes so much energy, time, and concentration that all too often growers give their all to the growing and too little to the marketing. This book is written to cure that problem. And I think it does.

"At the beginning of each market day I crush fresh basil and drop it in my shirt pocket so I'll smell like a farmer. I know it sounds silly, but try it sometime. I got this tip from a retired market gardener in Concord, Mass. I'm convinced I sell more basil and tomatoes because of it. Besides, I like the smell. It helps to cover body odors after a few hours in the sun, and it makes me feel good about myself and it's a soothing remedy to the hectic pace of the market day." That's Andy Lee, grower, author, consultant and executive director of the Intervale Foundation in Burlington, VT. (See listing under consultants.)

Cornucopia, A Source Book of Edible Plants, by Stephen Facciola. Kampong Publications, Vista, CA, 1990.

A grand reference book written for "gardeners, small-scale and alternative farmers, researchers, cooks, economic botanists, genetic preservationists, natural food enthusiasts, nutritionists, those in the specialty and gourmet food business, and colleges and universities." The point of the book is to fill in the huge gap that exists between the number of edible crops available to mankind (estimated at something like fifteen thousand) and the tiny number of crops (as few as twenty) that constitute the main food crops of the world. The joy of the book is to open up to an entry like basil and find more than 30 entries describing taste, growing habits, uses, and where to find the seeds and/or plants, even the fresh produce or food products. This is 700 pages of delicious reading. I talked my library into ordering this unusual book for the reference section. Perhaps you could do that, too.

Culinary Herbs, A Potpourri, James A Duke, Chief, Germplasm Resources Laboratory, USDA. Trado-Medic Books, New York, 1985.

A thorough introduction to the culinary herbs, their culture, culinary and folk medicine uses, written by one of America's best known herbalists. Gives herb-blend suggestions; informative chapters on herbal teas and liqueurs—including what herbs are used in commercial liqueurs. Charts showing vitamins and nutritional analysis of culinary herbs plus information on lots of wild greens. Lists of herbs for all uses and conditions: aphrodisiacs to witchcraft, dyes to narcotics. An excellent small reference work. Written with humor and a constant, wry disclaiming: he certainly doesn't think anyone should count on "being cured by herbs." Duke beckons you into the herb world with fascinating information, great humor, and stories from herbal lore.

Everlasting Flowers For Pleasure and Profit, by Jeanne Verhelst, PO Box 178, Radville, Sask., S0C 2G0, Canada.

Planting and harvesting, plus pricing, marketing, packing, and shipping of dried flower material.

Flowers For Sale: Growing & Marketing Cut Flowers, Backyard To Small Acreage, by Lee Sturdivant.

An introduction to the cut flower business including a list of flowers to grow for drying. See order coupon at the end of this book.

Greenhouse Engineering, by Aldrich and Bartock, Univ. of Conn., 1990.

A book recommended by several growers, for those wanting to build a new greenhouse.

Growing and Using Herbs Successfully, by Betty E. M. Jacobs. Storey Publications, Vermont, 1981.

One of the earliest and best guides for backyard commercial growers. Especially good on propagation and other important horticultural techniques.

Growing Great Garlic, by Ron Engeland. Filaree Productions. Available from Filaree Productions, Rt. 1, Box 162, Okanogan, WA 98840, for $12.95 plus $2 p&h.

See the chapter on garlic for more information on this fine book.

Herbal Bounty, by Steven Foster. Peregrine Books, 1984.

A splendid introductory book to growing and using herbs—if you can find it. Packed with unusual bits of information on special drying and harvesting techniques, culinary and medicinal usage. A small book, full of more information than many much larger volumes. Foster is a clear-thinking writer, with long experience in the world of herbs, both in the field and in research. I heard recently that Foster has just come out with a new, enlarged version titled, ***Herbal Renaissance,*** published by Peregrine-Smith, Utah. I would recommend it, sight unseen.

Kitchen Herbs, Sal Gilbertie, Bantam Books, New York, 1988

Written by one of the country's largest commercial herb growers. Lots of growing information, plus a real understanding of uses for fresh and dried herbs in the kitchen. Essays on each herb tell how to use it in every possible way. In the section on fennel, for instance, you'll learn how to use the hollow stalks, the tiny flower blossoms, the seeds, the thinly sliced root, **and** the greenery. How to keep herbs, store herbs, and use, use, use herbs. Also, recipes by the score for each and every herb Very meat, fish and poultry oriented. Recipes for herb oils and herbal vinegars.

Park's Success With Herbs, Park Seed Co., Greenwood, SC, 1980.

Excellent basic guide for cultivation of herbs. A to Z listing with close-up photographs to help you learn to recognize herb seedlings.

Profits From Your Backyard Herb Garden, by Lee Sturdivant.

More detailed information for beginning commercial herb and edible flower growers. See order coupon at the end of this book.

The Potential of Herbs as a Cash Crop, by Richard Alan Miller. Halcyon House, 1985.

Written by a commercial herb farmer, with details on propagation and harvest, bulk dehydration, storage, processing, etc. For serious farming efforts, it includes capital investment information and marketing techniques.

Southern Herb Growing, by M. Hill and G. Barclay. Shearer Publication, Fredericksburg, TX, 1987.

A good guide for dealing with some of the problems that can occur when trying to grow herbs in the south. Also includes recipes from a well known herb restaurant at Hilltop Herb Farm in Texas.

Specialty Cut Flowers: The Production of Annuals, Perennials, Bulbs and Woody Plants for Fresh and Dried Cut Flowers, by Alan M. Armitage. Timber Press, Portland, OR, 1993.

Armitage is considered one of the country's foremost authorities on commercial specialty cut flower production. Excellent information on harvesting and post-harvest handling of flowers, including those for drying.

The Herb Garden, by Sarah Garland. Viking Penguin, New York, 1984.

A good introduction to herbs, their history, uses and cultivation. There have been so many herb books published since this one came out, but I think it is still one of the nicest general guides to growing herbs in your garden.

RECOMMENDED MAIL ORDER HERB PLANT AND SEED SOURCES

Abundant Life Seed Foundation, PO Box 772, Fort Townsend, WA 98368. Cat. $1 (S)

Companion Plants, 7247 N. Coolville Ridge, Athens, OH 45701. Cat. $2 (S&P)

Comstock, Ferre & Co., PO Box 126, Wethersfield, CT 06109. Cat. $1 (S)

The Cook's Garden, PO Box 535, Londonderry, VT 05148. Cat. $1 (S)

Elixir Farm Botanicals, Elixir Farm, Brixey, MO 65618. Cat. $1 (S)

Fedco Seeds Co-op, 52 Mayflower Hill Dr., Waterville, ME 04901. Cat. free (S)

Flowery Branch Seed Co., PO Box 1330, Flowery Branch, GA 30542. Cat. $2 (S)

Forestfarm, 990 Tetherow Road, Williams, OR 97544. Cat. $3 (P)

Fox Hill Farm, Box 9, Parma, MI 49269. Cat. $1 (P)

Goodwin Creek Gardens, PO Box 83, Williams, OR 97544. Cat. $1 (S&P)

Herbs Liscious, 1702 S. 6th St., Marshalltown, IA 50158. Cat. $2 (P)

It's About Thyme, PO Box 878, Manchaca, TX 78652. Cat. $1 (P)

Johnny's Selected Seeds. Foss Hill Road, Albion, ME 04910. Cat. free (S)

Liberty Seed Co., PO Box 808, New Philadelphia, OH 44663. Cat. free (S)

Logee's Greenhouses, 141 North St., Danielson, CT 06239. Cat. $3 (P)

Nichols Garden Nursery, 1190 No. Pacific Hwy., Albany, OR 97321. Cat. free (S&P)

Park Seeds, Greenwood, SC 29647. Cat. free (S&P)

Pinetree Garden Seeds, Route 100, New Gloucester, ME 04260. Cat. free (S)

Plants of the Southwest, Agua Fria, Rt. 6, Box 11A, Santa Fe, NM 87501. Cat. $1.50 (S&P)

Redwood City Seed Co., PO Box 361, Redwood City, CA 94064. Cat. $1 (S)

Richters, Box 26, Goodwood, Ont., Canada L0C 1A0. Cat. $2.50 (S)

Sandy Mush Herb Nursery, 316 Surrett Cove Rd., Leicester, NC 28748-9622. Cat. $4 (S&P)

Seeds Blüm, Idaho City Stage, Boise, ID 83706. Cat. $3 (S)

Seeds of Change, 1364 Rufina Circle #5, Santa Fe, NM 87501. Cat. $3 (S)

Shepherd's Garden Seeds, 6116 Highway 9, Felton, CA 95018. Cat. $1 (S)

Stokes Seeds, Inc., PO Box 548, Buffalo, NY 14240. Cat. free. (S)

Sunrise Oriental Seed Co., PO Box 10058, Elmwood, CT. 06110. Cat. $1 (S)

Taylor's Herb Gardens, Inc. 1535 Lone Oak Rd., Vista, CA 92084. Cat. $3 (P)

Well-Sweep Herb Farm, 317 Mt. Bethel Rd., Port Murray, NJ 07865. Cat. $2 (S&P)

HERB FARMS

The size and location of your land,

the amenities of the Herb Farm itself,

the size of the commitment to be made,

even the hours of operation, can be so

varied that almost anyone can

consider such an operation.

Herb Farms

Herbs are becoming amazingly popular now all across the land. One of the main reasons for that continued popularity has got to be the growing network of Herb Farms everywhere. They are like little herb headquarters in every region of the country, putting out the good word on herbs, teaching and touting, supplying and servicing the ever growing demand for these useful plants. Herb Farm visiting is a lovely pastime—I recommend it. Now there are even directories listing Herb Farms and other businesses across the country (see page 115). I wouldn't leave home without one.

Time after time we found that new Herb Farms get started and developed because the owners became inspired after visits to still other Herb Farms. But instead of a big replication of similar Herb Farms everywhere, we have been amazed to find the contrast and variety offered to the herb hungry public. The offerings might include afternoon teas, or even meals or overnight accommodations; classes, lectures, and demonstrations of all sorts; gathering places for weddings or parties; picnic grounds for all to enjoy, or even nature hikes nearby. And, almost always, fine gardens to walk through, admire and learn from, shops full of herbs and herbal products to browse through and buy from.

The following chapters are intended to show you some of that endless variety of Herb Farms that are operating successfully around the country, and to help you think of possibilities for your own Herb Farm, if that should be your bent. I hope you will realize that there aren't any basic rules to follow (other than a love of herbs and a willingness to deal cheerfully with the public in some ways). The size and location of your land, the amenities of the Herb Farm itself, the size of the commitment to be made, even the hours of operation, can be so varied that almost anyone can consider such an operation.

Of course the amount of money you can earn from any small business is almost always dependent on the amount of time and commitment you can give to it. But often, we've found, small herb businesses are wanted as just a part time, even a weekend operation. I had a call recently from a young author, Jennifer Bayse, who is writing a book called *Weekend Entrepreneur*. I think her title exactly captures a portion of the small business interest these days.

"We have jobs (or incomes) that are almost enough, but we'd like to add to them. "

"I want to stay home with my young children, but I want to be earning some money at the same time."

"I started a small herb business because I want to retire (or quit) one of these days, and get into something else."

Almost all of the businesses in this book can be seen in that part-time light, but most can also be grown up to be full-time excellent-income businesses.

Let us take a look, then, at some varied Herb Farms around the country. See if you can see yourself in any of these operations.

Windbeam Herb Garden, Vermont

IF YOU ARE living in the city or suburbs right now, and yearning to try a more rural life, you'll appreciate the effort the Ciminos are making to build up Windbeam Herb Garden in Stowe, Vermont. Peter and Nanette spent the first part of their lives in New Jersey, as insurance claims adjusters. They are both still insurance adjusters, but they commute now almost an hour each way from Stowe, in order to keep their incomes high while they make this transition towards a business of their own and a lifestyle they both love.

Stowe is one of those picturesque tiny ski villages whose streets plug up daily with cars and tour buses, whose permanent residents must go nearly insane with all the visitations. Just a mile or two outside of the town, the lovely vistas open up again, and the reason for its fame becomes obvious. Soon the great charm of the place itself takes over completely. This is the area where the Ciminos bought a three bedroom home on 12 acres and set about turning it into the place of their dreams.

In their first three years in Vermont, they have put in magnificent herb and vegetable gardens on their acreage, established a very small retail shop adjoining the house, and then proceeded to fill it with herbal wares they have produced themselves: vinegars and spice mixes, potpourris, dried flower bouquets, swags and herbal wreaths, plus Peter's colorful herb and vegetable paintings on the walls. Yet, every weekday morning, month in and month out, they leave the gardens, the shop, two Suffolk sheep, four cats, three horses, two African goslings, an orange Amazon parrot, and their handsome Airedale dogs, climb into their car and drive the 35 miles to Williston and their insurance company jobs. In the evenings, and especially on weekends, they immerse themselves in what they love: growing and messing about with herbs.

In New Jersey they lived on a city lot that, by the time they left for Vermont, had not an open spot unplanted. Digging in the soil, they both say, is the greatest relief from their fairly high stress jobs. Leaving those jobs and turning their new life into a full-time reality is their aim.

The problems are considerable. First of all, Vermont, which I consider to be one of the most beautiful states in America, also has some of the strictest laws in the land on the environment. (Which is no doubt why it is still so beautiful.) Almost no signs are allowed on the Cimino property. They pay the state $60 a year for the small sign identifying the turn-off to their farm, a half mile ahead on the road. Then it is up to the sharp-eyed driver to find the place with only the tiniest of signs to help. On the day we visited, the Ciminos had a little (six-inch) wind sock attached to their mailbox; a neighbor had just reported them for that violation and now they would have to remove it.

They feel they can't afford to hire people to work in the shop yet, so everything is closed up, except on the weekends, when both work like crazy to build towards the dream. Each day they tell each other: "One of us has to quit that job and make this happen." A major problem is deciding which one gets to quit first. Both volunteer for that career change every time the subject is mentioned.

In the meantime, they are slowly building up a little weekend business and learning more about which direction to take. Right now, Nanette, who adores cooking with herbs, is trying her hand at cooking herbal lunches on one of the weekend days. They do a little advertising in the local paper—once they even tried the radio—and wait to see who shows up. This, after spending the better part of a year and quite a bit of money in getting local and state approval to do the lunches. This weekend's lunch menu sounds fabulous: eggplant Provencàle for appetizer, followed by fall harvest soup, chicken tarragon, marinated cucumbers, carrots with shallots and tarragon, tea and lemon tea bread for dessert. All this, plus a tour of the garden and the total attention of the Ciminos, for seventeen dollars. Some days several people have come; one day only one came. When that happens the rest of the food goes into the freezer to feed the Ciminos for the week. "And I love to do it," says Nanette. "I am learning soooooo much."

At one point they even hired a consultant to give them some hints on getting and keeping more weekend business. That led to their starting a guest book and doing a little newsletter with lots of herbal information and recipes. They both appreciate how much herbal educating they are doing. "Whenever we give recipes," says Nanette, "we always sell more of that herb. People are wanting to learn more and more about herbs, and we both spend lots of time just talking with people."

The Horticulture Society of California has already put the Windbeam Garden on their yearly tour, but most bus tours prefer weekday rather than weekend stops. Also, most tourists to the area come and go on weekends, leaving the local weekend business possibilities a little bare. But this slow beginning has also given the Ciminos lots of time to learn what they are doing, what they want to emphasize, and what will really pay off for them once they take the chance and quit their jobs for good.

Among their best selling products are the attractive little bottles of vinegars that Nanette has taught herself (from books) to make. She buys white wine vinegar by the gallon from a discount grocer, washes off the herbs she wants to use, pats them dry, then adds them (in fairly large quantities) to gallon jars, which she then fills with vinegar and sets in the sun for two to four weeks—or until much of the color has drained from the herbs.

She then pours the vinegar through a very fine strainer into ten ounce sterilized bottles. For decoration, she adds a bit of freshly washed and patted-dry herbs, using chopsticks to push the herbs down into the bottle. She corks the bottle with a cork she has purchased from the local hardware store, seals it with melted paraffin, and attaches a tiny little picot ribbon bow around the neck of the bottle, before adding the Windbeam label. It makes a very handsome, small souvenir and appears to be easy to carry, because of the paraffin. The price is only $3.95, so most visitors take at least one bottle home. Their best selling vinegar is the one made with opal basil that turns the vinegar a luscious shade of cranberry.

They keep trying new herbal taste blends, both for the vinegars and for their little packets of dried herb mixes that also sell very well. These are items people can carry along easily, know

Purple opal basil vinegar from Windbeam Herb Garden

they will use at home, and that also make souvenir gifts to take to others. The packs of single herbs don't sell all that well, says Nanette, but her blends, like Boursin Cheese Blend, or Poultry Blend, do very well. They retail for only $2.50 each. The Ciminos' prices are still rather low compared to other, more established Herb Farms.

Peter's long term plan now envisions a small bed and breakfast when they can get the time and all the permits required. Nanette's short term dream is to be able to quit soon and do more at the farm. "Cooks should stay home first," she says to Peter, probably for the hundredth time this week. Meanwhile, they are looking at plans for a greenhouse, selling their vinegars at a local produce stand on the highway, looking to put herbs in the natural food market in town, supplying one town chef with herbs occasionally, and planning on inviting all the local innkeepers for a lunch. At the time of our visit, they were making time to prepare the gardens for the 30 to 50 inches of snow that will start to arrive within a few weeks. All this while they keep their full-time jobs and daily commutes.

The Ciminos decided to try for an Herb Farm of their own after visiting the well known Caprilands Herb Farm in Connecticut, probably one of the most renowned Herb Farms in the country. If an Herb Farm might be in your future, I suggest you make a point to visit every Herb Farm and nursery in your area, or anywhere you travel in the country. If your travels should take you to Vermont, it's worth a trip out of your way to go to Stowe to check in on the Ciminos, and to watch them bring their dreams home.

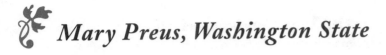

Mary Preus, Washington State

A GOOD THREE thousand miles from the Cimino farm, near Bremerton, Washington, on Puget Sound, Mary Preus has accomplished some of what the Ciminos are trying. Her Herb Farm is one of my very favorite places; please come there on this visit with me. From the busy road that runs through Silverdale, near Bremerton, we drive down a winding dirt driveway that stops when you reach the herb gardens. The herb gardens stop only when they reach the silvery waters of Dyes Inlet on the Sound.

Western Washington state is a fast growing area where the sense of the place that *was* Washington is fast disappearing. Yet that sense of distinctive place is still very much a part of Silver Bay Herb Farm, and a part of what makes it so appealing: an old house with barns and outbuildings sitting right on the waterfront, ancient Douglas fir and oak trees that tower over everything. Nothing slick, nothing very up-scale, everything old, peaceful, and comforting. There are gardens everywhere, filled with herbs and flowers, with the shimmering water of the bay as a backdrop to all. The property has been in Mary's family for a long time, but this is Mary's dream we are visiting—a dream based on a passion for herbs.

The location is definitely out of the way; you would only stumble on it by chance. They sell lots of potted herbs and fresh cut culinary herbs to all comers, including local restaurants. There is a tiny, very fragrant herb shop full of elegant herbal products, many of which Mary has made. These are the basic, almost everyday attractions of the farm. Mary has taught lots of classes, sold herbs to supermarkets, and done many other herbal endeavors over the years trying to improve her business.

For years she traveled every week across Puget Sound by ferry to sell her herbal products at the Pike Place Market, the fabulous farmers' market known throughout the country. She also made a lot of contacts selling herbs to the best restaurant chefs in Seattle during those years and, through those friendships, was able to develop an idea that has now made her Herb Farm one of the most unique and better known in the area; an idea that has now allowed her to stay home more with her family and tend the herbs and gardens she loves.

A few years ago when a posh garden shop asked if they could bring their customers to the farm, they also asked Mary if she could provide a place for those on the tour to have a picnic. They brought their own chef, spread quilts on the lawn and proceeded to have one very fine time on the shores of the bay, surrounded by Mary's bountiful herb gardens. Of course, they bought lots of things from the shop, too, as most touring customers do. The chef happened to be one whom Mary had been supplying with herbs over the years, so the following year she invited him to come back and put on a "Gourmet Herbal Picnic" at Silver Bay Herb Farm. Mary has been building on this idea ever since and pleasing lots of people (including me) who can make it to one of her incredible events. Because Mary doesn't just get a cook for

Pavilion at Silver Bay Herb Farm, on Puget Sound

these events—she features five or six of the very best chefs in the U.S., who happen to be working in the Seattle area at the time.

Barbara Figueroa, for instance, winner of the James Beard Foundation Award for Best Chef of the Northwest in 1992, came that same year to cook a picnic at Mary's. Last summer I attended a picnic featuring Kerry Sear, Executive Chef of the Four Seasons Olympic Hotel, one of Seattle's highest rated hotels and restaurants. It was unlike any other picnic I have ever attended.

The picnics are held under a 24'x24' pavilion on the sand near the water; the rustic tables are covered with white linen and bouquets; Mary's friends and a young employee help serve. Chef Sear gathered everyone around his preparation tables and the two barbecues near the pavilion and proceeded to talk to the guests about the meal he would be offering, describing the preparation of the food and his use of the herbs from Mary's gardens. He told his own little herbal cooking secrets, demonstrating them as we all watched with delighted interest. He answered questions, told funny stories and, after a bit, everyone sat happily down to eat.

The menu featured a lavish salad made up primarily of herbs, greens, and edible flowers picked from the nearby gardens and dressed with subtly flavored olive oil. Next came *Fire Roasted Leg of Lamb With Wild Currant Relish, Roasted Potatoes On Rosemary Skewers, Vegetable Steak With Indian Spice Butter, Espresso Mousse in Chocolate Coffee Cups.* Plus lots of herb teas, of course, and all served elegantly in these simple, rustic surroundings—the secret, I think, to this special affair. That combination of truly well prepared food served, not only without fuss and fanfare, but in nearly primitive, yet visually gorgeous surroundings, is simply a knockout to the senses. Unexpected, yet perfectly right.

After the meal, there are tours of the gardens given by Mary. Friendly, informative, inviting. Mary's passion for the herbs shines through in all she does. I'm certain almost everyone leaves with the same thought I have: who shall I bring here next season to enjoy these wonderful picnics?

Mary has about six picnics per year and charges $25 for each of them. In between she also brings fine bakers to the farm for tea parties. She charges $12 to $15 for those events. She also gives a Teddy Bear Tea for adults and children, ages three to 12. For this she charges $6 for adults and $4 for children. These events, combined with regular classes of potpourri or vinegar making, family herbal remedies, soap making, etc., make up a full season and help keep Mary on the farm and close to the raising of her daughters, Miriam, 12, and Eve, 15. She sends out a little newsletter each spring to announce all the picnics, tea parties, and classes for the year, and to tell bits of news about the farm.

"Herb Farms," says Mary, "are a lot of work; both mental and physical work. Plus lots of pencil pushing. In order to actually make an Herb Farm work you have to do a lot of thinking. A lot of trying of different things, perhaps, but always working towards your long term goals."

Her advice to other Herb Farm people who might want to try an herbal luncheon or picnic like hers is both generous and quite specific:

Every chef (and their restaurant), says Mary, may want a different arrangement for staging such an event as the Gourmet Picnic. At the Silver Bay, chefs generally provide the menu, food, cooking tips, recipes and any cooking assistants, if needed. The farm provides the atmosphere, picnic tables, herbal teas, fresh herbs and flowers, garden tours, serving assistant(s) and the publicity and guests. Mary says that the negotiable things are usually dishes, table linens, and silverware. She has plenty of all of these but some chefs prefer to bring their own. The price, too, is negotiable, she says, both in what to charge and how much goes for food, labor, publicity, preparation, etc. "High profile, out of town chefs," she says, "may receive a larger percentage than local chefs."

Mary requires a reservation and a 50% deposit from her customers at least a week in advance. Deposits are transferable if someone can't make it, but not refundable. "You get more firm about this as you lose money when your guests don't show up." She collects the balance due on the day of the picnic.

Mary's publicity is done through her newsletter/announce-
ments which go out to about fifteen hundred potential customers. She also distributes them through the local Visitor and
Convention Bureau and the Chamber of Commerce offices. She
sends press releases to the local and regional papers, and posts
the picnic menus at her farm for all visitors to see.

Bremerton, the main town nearby, is truly a "lunch bucket"
town—long the site of U. S. Naval shipyards and installations.
Not a town, you would think, that could supply 25 to 40 people
for a weekday lunch costing $25. That's where Mary's deter-
mined efforts on publicity have paid off. The picnic I went to
was well attended by a group of visiting assessors who were staying at a small convention/hotel center in Silverdale. The Chamber of Commerce had asked the local businesses to supply
welcoming souvenirs to the visitors; when Mary sent along her
little herbal gift, she also included an invitation to her next gourmet picnic. The assessors turned out in force, and loved every
minute of it.

In working out the menus with the chefs, Mary keeps in mind
that her main criterion is "a gourmet meal featuring fresh herbs."
But sometimes that part of the planning can be a little tricky.

"One chef," she recalls, "suggested a Sea Urchin Sauce. Remember, I said, this is Silverdale. Is this really appropriate?

"If it weren't appropriate, I wouldn't serve it, he said, with fi-
nality.

"I said, wellllll, okay. He served it and it was superb and everyone loved it. Chefs definitely are the experts on food. Something like calamari salad might be left on plates untouched, but
most people who come to such an event are willing to try something new."

Mary has found that most (though not all) chefs love to come
and work for such an informal, up-close gathering, and that most
customers really appreciate close encounters with famous chefs.
It still amazes and delights her that "the aura of glamour and
success that my customers associate with these top chefs has
somehow been transferred to my humble business!" She has no-

ticed that top chefs nowadays get lots of newspaper, magazine, and television publicity about their personal lives, their homes, even their wardrobes. "Chefs are glamorous," says Mary, "at least to people who don't hang around kitchens."

She advises anyone who wants to try such an adventure to start small, and don't try to tackle too much at once. Keep a very sharp pencil, she encourages, and figure everything out ahead of time that you possibly can. Remember, of course, that much can go wrong: the weather, sick chefs, not enough guests signed up, not enough food, too much food and no doggie bags, a clogged toilet, beverages or food spilled on guests, arrival of neighborhood dogs. The list of possibilities, she says, is endless. "My best advice," she smiles, "is to think things through, do what you can to prepare, and remain calm. If things go crazy, just tell yourself, this too will pass."

Mary's new schedule should be arriving soon. Who will she bring in this year? Can I get away to attend more than one picnic? Should I indulge myself so much? Is there anyone who would dare to stop me?

Meadowsweet Farm, Vermont

"YOU HAVE TO create something in someone's mind that makes them want to come. And then want to come back." That's Polly Haynes on one of the secrets to creating a great Herb Farm.

If I had to send every reader to only one location to learn about Herb Farms, I might very well choose Shrewsbury, Vermont, and the handsome work of Polly and Elliott Haynes,

New England villages are surely the perfect setting for some of America's best known Herb Farms. The villages lend lots of charm to the businesses that locate in them, and the businesses themselves, like Meadowsweet Farm at Shrewsbury, make visits to the little village even more desirable. But beyond the appeal of New England are the years and years of intensive work and creativity that have gone into the Meadowsweet experience. It's Polly's experience, actually, and one worth learning from.

Polly and Elliott both worked in Manhattan, she in publishing at Doubleday, he in international publishing that required only that he be near a telephone and an airport. They decided to bail out of the city in the '60s and they moved to rural Connecticut, where she went to work at Yale and also made her first trip with her herb-loving grandmother to Caprilands, the now famous Herb Farm of Adelma Simmons. Polly said she so loved the place that she began to "hang out there all the time, learning all I could. Elliott realized I'd become totally hooked on herbs when I named our golden retrievers Tansy and Teasle."

In 1976, they moved permanently to a Vermont farm in the mountain hamlet of Shrewsbury, near where they'd had a weekend home since 1969. Polly immediately set about moving her herbs from Connecticut. The big old white farmhouse itself was built in 1860, replete with ballroom. But it is six miles from any main road in all directions, and there is only one other business in the village of 900 people—not a place one should ever consider as a good location, location, location, for a potential business. Unless you're Polly Haynes and totally hooked on herbs.

"This was corn and tomato country," she says. "No one seemed to have heard of herbs up here. Connecticut was so English, so herby, but this was really Italian and French Canadian country and totally different."

They built a tiny solar greenhouse attached to the house, where Polly grew all the herbs she could, and then began selling herbs at farmers' markets and at the farm in 1978. She ran the house and basement full of fluorescent lights in order to grow more plants but she could only grow enough to sell for two months. The demand just kept increasing. She'd found something people in the area were wanting to know about, she had boundless energy and enthusiasm for teaching and, over the years, Polly turned the farm, and their lives, into a full-time, highly successful Herb Farm in the classic style. In the early days her farm became famous for its wreaths, swags, and dried flower arrangements. To this day they still turn out tussie mussies and bouquets for weddings that I swear most brides would prefer to fresh flowers, so perfect are the arrangements. And, of course, these bouquets will keep indefinitely—something very desirable for remembering special occasions. In fact, they still do "ship weddings all over the country" a couple of times a month.

Her first employee for the farm was a gardener, who could also learn to make handsome wreaths. She still hires and trains only local folks. I think it is Polly's ability to train people to do both these and other jobs very well that is one big secret to the success of Meadowsweet. She has a fine sense of design and proportion, and the confidence to teach, with great patience, as much as her employees can possibly absorb. The farm itself probably draws the very best from the area for employees. The employees sign their name on a little decorative Meadowsweet tag that attaches to each wreath or swag, thus getting credit (and responsibility) for the work they do.

Another hallmark of the farm is friendliness. A large pond with inviting lawns sits behind the house; visitors are invited to

Shaker barn, Meadowsweet Farm

bring their picnics and share this lovely landscape. "People who have the luxury of owning one of these old hand-crafted homes ought to share it with other people," says Polly, who firmly believes that a large part of her job is to help her employees find ways to remain friendly to people no matter how many folks pile in. We all know that familiar "we/they" pattern that develops in many businesses dealing with the public. Constantly serving the public can be difficult indeed, and worn out employees often end up stressed and defensive with the customers—who can suddenly seem like the enemy. Polly works hard to keep that attitude out of Meadowsweet entirely.

"You have to control your own mind," she says, "so that you can meet that commitment you've made to the public. I try to keep a bit of a party atmosphere going on the farm to help my employees share that feeling of guests and visitors, not just customers—no matter how many pour in here."

And pour in they do: cars and tour buses full of people wanting a day in the country, out of the city and suburbs, touching base with that rural heritage lodged deep in the soul of all of us.

The Herb Farm as Rural Experience—Meadowsweet is the perfect example of that. You can take a short walk from the farm in all directions and see where all the pictures of rural New England must surely come from: the softly rolling hills, the church spires in the distance, the narrow, unfinished roads that keep people slowed down and attentive to their surroundings; the excellence of a place that enriches your life just by walking or driving through it. It's all there around Meadowsweet. And then some. Polly, from Manhattan, is completely aware of this need in people and honors it.

"They tell us how important the air and water quality are here. They love being reminded of another, more beautiful life: English, Victorian, rural—it's part of a dream that Herb Farms create in everyone's head. If you want to build an Herb Farm, never forget that part of it. That's what keeps them coming back. The dream part." This is also the way Polly deals with her very out-of-the-way location. "It's foolish to present yourself in a negative way. You have to present yourself so that this out-of-the-way location is a positive part of the experience. And it is."

So many people have returned to Meadowsweet so many times that a few years ago they built a magnificent Shaker barn across the road from the house, and moved the business over there. With the building of the barn, Elliott and Polly regained almost all of their home to live in again. "The dining room had become the UPS shipping room, the kitchen had become the employee lounge; employees were working in almost every room in the house."

The original smaller shop adjoining the house still carries all the Meadowsweet products: herb seeds, herb blends and party dips, potpourri, scented hot pads, herb vinegars, books on herbs, and specialty food items from Vermont. The herb blends and party dips were the very first farm products at Meadowsweet, and all visitors to the shop are invited to taste the dips which are daily mixed in sour cream and set around the shop with crackers. Small herb packets are incredibly good sellers at almost every farm we visited. Meadowsweet was no exception. Polly's

Basic Blend, "*a savory blend of nine herbs which we use daily at the farm,*" comes in a small four ounce spice jar with a cork stopper, and sells for $3.

Another product that does well by mail, and with tourists, are the little Meadowsweet herb seed packets. The packets have one basic design with printed names for only the most popular herbs, and rubber stamps used for the others. Each packet has "*over 100 seeds,*" and costs $1.25. These are easily carried and make a welcome gift to take home. Polly purchases most seeds in bulk and repackages them at the farm.

Putting in the new barn building across the road also meant that the primary gardens had to be moved, and that major project was still being done at the time of our visit. Polly recognizes more interest than ever these days in gardening and is reconstructing several theme gardens to include heirloom fruit and vegetable gardens, again sensing an interest in such things by those who visit the farm. She seems to have almost a sixth sense about where the public in her region is headed in their thinking—and how to stay ahead of that curve in her own business. The barn has now been turned into a workroom/classroom for demonstrations and craft classes. The dried flower crafts are better for teaching these days, she believes, than for selling.

The success of Meadowsweet has allowed Polly the luxury of being able to think a lot about the farm and where it is going, something many small business owners seldom get enough time to do. But thinking about your business direction, really thinking about it—seriously and often—is something almost all successful business people mention as very important to their success. Instead, it's easy to get bogged down in the day to day operations and *stacking all the bottles ourselves*, so that we can miss major changes or opportunities.

Polly advertises regularly in the *Herb Companion* magazine, maintains a mailing list of over 25,000 people, and advertises in local newspapers. Like many other New England craft and herb businesses, she (or others from the farm) also attends a series of craft shows all over New England. They occur from April to December, are held indoors and out, and Meadowsweet Farm participates in up to 18 shows a year. These craft shows and herb show/festivals have become big business in the country because they not only draw large retail crowds, but because many shop owners seek out new and unusual suppliers at these shows in an effort to please the changing tastes of their ever more sophisticated customers. In New England, the craft show tradition is the strongest in the country, although other areas (including my own Pacific Northwest) are showing greater interest all the time.

In 1993 Meadowsweet began a new weekend celebration at the farm called, "A Taste of Herbs Open House." Polly enlisted the aid of a young French-trained chef, and between them they put on great herb tasting parties in the kitchen and dining room of the old farmhouse:

"Visitors to the farmhouse will be able to taste a variety of herbal refreshments prepared with fresh herbs and edible flowers including soups, breads, dressings, butters, sauces, pasta, pesto, vinegars, punch and more," read the newspaper articles about the open house events, which were then held weekends all during the summer and fall.

They give tours of the gardens and on-going demonstrations on the use of herbs in the kitchen, for crafts, and in simple home remedies. They don't charge for the open house, which draws big crowds, and creates ever more publicity for the farm.

Visitors get little recipe booklets for quick and simple ways to use herbs: "Everyone's getting a garden full of herbs," says Polly, "and what they need are some jump-starts into learning how to use them." She offers Quick Rosemary Marmalade, Quick Rose Geranium Jelly, Easy Herb Butters, Quick Herb Mustards, and a dozen other almost instant herb tastes to help people make that transition to the use of herbs in their cooking.

Once people make the trip to Meadowsweet Farm, become inspired, and see the quality of the work, they then order easily from the catalog feeling confident about what will arrive. Polly spends much of her time training to what she calls "a look" in the farm's creations. She starts any non-gardening employee out as a weeder in the gardens, knowing for certain that only by working with live blossoms can dried floral arrangers understand how finished floral products can look. It is this strong connection to the garden that she thinks keeps the designs freshest. She doesn't use materials treated with dyes or glycerine, preferring to stay with a more natural look. She also tries to work only with materials that ship well (no hydrangea) and doesn't use fillers, such as Sweet Annie.

"Our main flowers are larkspur, roses, lavenders, clumps of fresh herbs; all things you would find growing in old-fashioned gardens." What they can't grow themselves Polly finds from suppliers all over the country and, sometimes, overseas. "Start with the ads in the *Business of Herbs*," she suggests, "and then stay on the phone or writing until you find what you want. And **always** ask for a sample. If the people you are talking to don't have what you are looking for, ask their advice, their suggestions." The herbal network, she believes, is a tight one and helpful at that.

The barn is the product center of the business. Wall shelves are stacked with bags of dried herbs, fruits, cones and berries: lemon verbena, larch cones, birch cones, malva flowers, globe amaranth flowers, roses, lavender, cloves, cinnamon sticks and chips, coriander seeds, rosemary leaves, hops, arrowroot, sesame seed, juniper berries, and on and on. Free-standing shelves are stacked with finished products.

I watched one morning as they prepared a batch of Berry Spice Potpourri—a bushel at a time. But no one watches too closely. As with most product makers, the actual farm recipes are held secret, and although careful examination of potpourri can reveal most of the ingredients, there is always that little something, that certain fragrance that can create the special quality customers want.

A lot of potpourri on the market these days is known as decorator potpourri: big chunks of dyed bark (or even cardboard) with added slices of dried fruit, pine cones, leaves or what have you. Meadowsweet specializes in the old fashioned varieties: Victorian Rose Geranium, Wild Rose, Balsam & Pine, and Old

Fashioned Lavender, to name a few. They seem to use lavender, roses and lemon verbena in almost every floral recipe. They also sell lots of Apple Cinnamon Potpourri, ever since the psychology department at Yale reported that the fragrance of Spiced Apples reduces stress.

Dot, who is working today, mixes the batch with a careful, light touch. "It will break up if you handle it too much," she says. "But it has to be mixed again just before you begin packaging." As she pours in the measuring cups of ingredients, she and Polly discuss the secrets of great potpourri.

"We make things look and smell a little lighter in the spring, maybe a little darker and heavier in the fall," says Dot.

"Potpourri makers have to educate their noses," says Polly, "just the way a wine or brandy expert, or a perfume expert, has to educate her nose. I recommend that people start educating their noses by going to fine shops and sniffing. Visit a Caswell-Massey shop and learn the power of fine aromas. And then get some books on potpourri recipes and start experimenting with little batches."

Dot gives a few sprays from a bottle of fragrant oils over the potpourri as she adds the ingredients. This oil, plus orris root, are the fixatives for this batch. Polly tries to decide if they should add juniper berries at this time of year. Yes, she thinks so. We move to the work tables to begin the packaging.

A new girl, Tammy, is being trained today, and several new packaging materials are being tried out. Here, says Polly, "is where real patience pays off. The packaging materials are one of the trickiest parts of this business—finding just the right package for each product. I spend a lot of my time on this—chasing after these little things. But it really pays off."

Polly stuffs one little cellophane bag and ties it with a ribbon. How does it look? she asks.

"All wrinkled, it looks like Wal-Mart," Tammy says, and they all laugh in agreement. Polly tries the next bag which is of a little different material, a slightly different shape. This time the potpourri fills out the bag smoothly, giving it uniform shape. It is amazing to see the very same product suddenly become something you'd expect to see at Saks Fifth Avenue, instead of a discount store.

"See," says Polly, "this one has the look of a little soft box. Classy, yet friendly." All because of a little cellophane package costing only a penny or two. They try different ribbons, with Tammy working now, learning to fill, tie and weigh the package, some with little bottles of fragrant oil inside to replenish the potpourri fragrance; some, less expensive packages, without the oil. Polly stands by gently encouraging, helping, explaining, always working everything and everyone towards what she calls that "look" of the farm: a sense of quality she believes her customers have come to trust and that gives her the confidence and pride of ownership in the place that is so evident to the visitor.

"We used to use a little rigid plastic box," she says, "but it just got looking so gifty, so unfriendly, that I switched to cellophane." These differences are so subtle—yet, as I watch, I can see how very important they are in the look of the final product. And in the price that can be charged.

The standard poodle, Lady Larkspur, comes in for her morning biscuit, and the talk turns to labeling information. Previously, Polly only showed the volume measurement on the labels. Then, at a New Jersey craft show, along came state inspectors and told her that she wouldn't comply with New Jersey regulations until she listed product weights on her label. They gave her a stern warning and then went to a man next to her, who was selling nuts using a scale that hadn't been recently checked, and gave him an instant thousand dollar fine. She now puts both volume and weight on her labels.

When Polly looks to the future, she sees people wanting to stay home more, wanting to learn more about lots of things, including herbs. She is feeling the same push we are all feeling from people wanting to learn more about herbal medicine and herbal remedies, and she plans to spend even more time on that.

The latest word from Meadowsweet is their effort to take some of their products, probably their vinegars and party dips, into a more national market. The state of Vermont has done a remarkable job in promoting the crafts of Vermont (black and white cows, included, of course). Polly Haynes now sees Meadowsweet Farm products in a tiny corner of that national picture we are all getting of "great stuff" coming from Vermont.

Meanwhile, Meadowsweet Farm operates seven days a week, from 10 AM to 5 PM, mid-May to late October. Get there if you can. I promise you a treat. Elliott will be there feeding the trout in the pond. Jack and Jill, the geese, will be there beside him. Take a lunch. Enjoy.

Summers Past Farms, San Diego

AS IMPORTANT AS dreams are for the making of a wonderful Herb Farm, the establishment itself will actually be formed and shaped by many things just as important as those dreams. Your reveries will start and first shape a new Herb Farm, but reality will always be there working its own magic. And daily, almost imperceptibly, the real world, as in the geography, the customers, the clock and your bank account, all will play very big roles in what actually develops on the land. A visit to the Summers Past Farms in Flinn Springs, California, is a pretty good example of a new Herb Farm taking shape from large inputs of both dreams and reality.

First of all, the land: four acres in San Diego County, where Marshall Lozier was born and raised, where he learned from his mother to grow tomatoes, beans and corn, and where, with his parents' encouragement, he also learned to raise calves and chickens and to sell the garden grown vegetables in his neighborhood. The land is still there, so is the cottage Marshall grew up in, but the neighborhood and the people of Southern California have changed completely during those 30 plus years during which Marshall went off to get educated, and then to do construction and landscaping work. Now Marshall and his wife Sheryl are working extremely hard to regain some of his remembered good life on that land while, at the same time, having to take into account the big changes that have come to the region that surrounds those four acres.

Sheryl, too, was raised in the San Diego County area, and then followed her own interest and education in cooking, working first as a line chef for Sheraton Hotel Restaurants, and then as a galley chef on fancy yachts along the east coast and in the Caribbean. She has set her cooking interests to the side for the moment and taken up gardening, nursery making, shop keeping, field work, small animal raising, and even crowd control in her efforts to make their new business come alive. Here are two very talented, hard working people watching their dream of a nice little farm business turn into something far more elaborate than either of them dreamed about.

They chose to call their little operation Summers Past Farms, in honor of the happy childhood spent on the land. They also chose to open only on weekends, hoping to work hard Monday through Thursday to raise enough vegetables and vegetable starts, plus herbs and perennials to sell on the three day weekends. The farm faces a frontage road that faces a freeway leading to the town of Julian, a very popular weekend getaway place for the now millions of people who live in San Diego County. In fact, the road is part of the so-called "Laguna Loop" leading into the Laguna mountains, written about in every tourist and traveler's guide to the area. On weekends it is jammed with cars going to and from the Julian area, and the Summers Past Farms sign and barn are easily seen from all the cars. The little weekend would-be farm-stop is quickly turning into a full blown and very popular Herb Farm. Sheryl had visited Caprilands Herb Farm on the east coast, but had not really seen the connection that wonderful place might have with this business in California. Now that connection is becoming ever stronger in her mind.

Instead of being interested in purchasing tomato starts, the hundreds who stop in at the farm every weekend are much more interested in walking out and gazing at the fields of flowers for drying that the Loziers have planted. They want to purchase herbs, large pots of them, to be used right away, and they want to learn to make things with all the dried flowers that the Loziers have hung in the beautiful barn. They love to buy every bird house that Marshall can find time to make, and the garden markers, the potted plants, the endless little sheaves of wheat that are grown and brought into the barn. Their interest in farm fresh vegetables is minimal, to say the least. Their interest in coming to the farm to tap into that rural experience that so many of them once knew, or want to know about, is boundless.

"They come once and then come again and again, bringing friends and relatives to just walk out in the flower fields and admire what we are doing," says Sheryl, amazed and delighted to see what their effort is turning into. Her big concerns of the day can now turn out to be having enough parking and bathrooms; having places for people to sit down and something for them to drink. "Things we never, ever thought of before," she says

They have calls all the time from garden clubs wanting to bring large groups to the farm, but they haven't quite figured out how to deal with that yet. The parking is a big problem, simply because the Loziers never thought they could create such a big draw with a little farm-stop idea, and made no special plans for parking.

Wholesale florists have come begging for their dried flowers. The Loziers quickly learned how much better they can do by offering those same blossoms as raw material for the wreath and swag making that Sheryl has learned herself, and is now teaching. She charges $35 for a three hour class on wreath making and the students take home their own 15" wreath, made almost exclusively with the blossoms grown there on the land. Sheryl has brought in dried rose buds, plus a few other blossoms, but primarily the wreaths are made with farm grown materials. So far, almost every class has filled up. A finished 15" wreath ordinarily sells for $39.95, so the classes are seen as a bargain.

One end of the barn is furnished with a long table and chairs for the classes. Dried flower bunches of every type and hue available are tacked to the wall near the tables. The students get up and clip off whatever they think they'd like to add to their wreath; the price includes the frame, all the material, use of the glue gun, and Sheryl's attentive help. She has enough room to handle 18 students at once, and when each class fills up with phone reservations, she simply adds another class. The swag class went from one to four classes the first time she offered it. She asks for a deposit to hold the class place open and, so far, nearly everyone has shown up. She has been amazed that almost no one else in the area is into teaching these crafts, and she plays into

Summers Past Farms,
Flinn Springs, California

the economic hard times of the area by encouraging people to make their own gifts.

"We started out during very hard times in this area," says Marshall. "Now I think we've come through the worst of the bad economy around here. We've done well enough this last year that I think we'll be OK in the future—if we can learn to handle all this OK," he says, spreading his arm out to include the fields, the barn and retail sales area.

Until now they have been making their own soil for the potted plants, but today Sheryl has their first bags of potting soil in the back of the truck. They are also now looking into buying pre-planted plugs for many of the plants. They get up at 5 AM every day to try and deal with their own lists of jobs to do, things to make, information to learn.

They own a large and small rototiller and a small John Deere tractor. Because of his own background in landscaping, Marshall knew how to install efficient, inexpensive automated watering and fertilizer systems in the fields. Like many others we have visited, they use the thin perforated Roberts tape hoses that sell for less than $200 for 12,000 feet. Marshall also built their 52"x96" propagation tables. So far, the only help they have hired has been to run the cash register on weekends.

The front part of the property includes big cages of fuzzy rabbits, small display gardens of herbs, flowers and vegetables plus tables filled with pots of scented geraniums, herbs, and yes, even some vegetable starts—although neither Sheryl nor Marshall now believes that vegetables are the key to the future of Summers Past Farms. During their first summer they grew hundreds of pounds of fresh, vine-ripened tomatoes, and were stunned to find that their customers asked for the little salad tomatoes they had grown used to purchasing at the local supermarket.

But they have offered a few classes in growing perennial gardens, taught by themselves or other local experts, and more than 50 local people have shown up to sit in the little shade houses and learn about perennials. These customers ask for flats of thyme and chamomile for lawn making. Sheryl and Marshall make them up and sell them for $35.

They knew that wheat sheaves would be popular, and checked out the prices at the local import shop. Their own price of $16 for a nice bunch undercuts the importer's price by six or eight dollars, and still makes a nice profit. They believe their own costs to be less than three or four dollars a bunch to grow, clean, and bunch the wheat.

Now they are looking into getting tee shirts printed up with their logo design because they recognize that "everyone seems to want a little piece of this operation." Sheryl has a list "a mile long" of things she wants to make that she knows will sell, like cat toys and some food items. She would also love to teach cooking. "Wouldn't a pasta festival be great? Maybe even a pasta cook-off. All this basil and tomatoes, some fresh bread. But really, it's too scary. Where would we put everyone? And all those cars?"

Although they only opened the farm in the fall of '92, by the following summer the Loziers realized they had built a far different operation than either of them first dreamed of. Now they are looking at the surrounding properties for places to park all the cars that show up, thinking of larger facilities to handle the people who want to come in groups, considering wild ideas like maybe an outdoor cafe (here comes Sheryl's still passionate interest in food) or even a micro-brewery. But there is still some hesitation in their voices, in their planning. They worked for two years to prepare this land for growing and now here are all these other possibilities taking them in far different directions.

They realize they have returned to a remarkable, now changed location (that was considered "way out in the boondocks" when Marshall was a boy) and that the customers, too, are much changed from those days of selling them tomatoes and zucchinis from a little wagon cart. But Marshall and Sheryl are also far different, I think, than business people of another era. They are not only hard working and energetic but have a worldliness about them that makes them able to adapt to whatever comes their way, once they make up their minds that they want what is probably going to be a very big business instead of the small one they dreamed of.

The local papers did brief stories on the farm opening and then the local slick magazines of the area picked up on the stories and came out to do three and four page color spreads of these handsome young people in the lovely environment they have created. That only increased the crowds and now they are constantly harassed on week days to "open up and let us in." So far they have resisted, needing those four days just to prepare for the onslaught of the weekends. The local television stations have called wanting to come out and do a piece on them, but they have resisted that, too.

They know they must adapt, and probably will, to accommodate this bigger dream—they just need a little more time to figure it all out. And they know that they cannot continue to do everything themselves: all the growing, all the product making, all the teaching, all the handling of customers. They also realize that they actually have two businesses. One is for the local area, providing plants and classes and information for neighborhood people. The other business, the one going by out there on the freeway, waiting and wanting to be lured off into their own summers past, is the scary one, and the one they were really not prepared for. But that one, of course, offers all the grand potential—once Marshall and Sheryl make up their own minds that that's the direction they really want to take.

I just received the winter issue of *Herb Companion* magazine. It has a full color, full page ad for Summers Past Farms, now open Wednesdays through Sundays. The Loziers, it seems, are making up their minds.

Jim Long, Missouri

I HOPE THE reader is getting the important idea that new Herb Farms are someone's cream waiting to happen—and that the dream must then adapt to the reality of the business world. No two people, of course, dream in the same way; it is the owner's personality and dreams that will give the farm its character and appeal. And it is the owner's personal needs and dreams that must be met in developing the farm. Your own plans have to evolve into something you can live with for the long term, something that reflects your own approach to life in very basic ways. Herb Farms are a big investment in work, time, and money, and a huge investment in commitment. One should not step casually up to the idea of an Herb Farm. But I do want to get across the idea that there is no formula. Whatever it is you could possibly dream up in this field, is no doubt possible and workable—as long as you bring along enough of those things: time, work, money, and commitment to your dream.

Which brings us all to the Ozarks and to Jim Long, and his own dreamy Long Creek Herb Farm. Sit down in the rocker here on his porch, close your eyes and listen to the farm animals (*are those guinea fowl I hear?*), smell the gardens (*that mint is so strong I must be rocking on it*) and enjoy the land all around you. (*I'm miles and miles from nowhere and it's more beautiful than anywhere.*) Sip a little freshly made herbal tea. If you stretch your neck you can almost see Table Rock Lake in the woods nearby. You are there now, in Jim Long's dream, and one of the most amazing things to know about it is that he only opens the farm to the public on **one midweek day each week.** If it's not Wednesday, don't head out to Long Creek Herb Farm. At least not without a phone call.

Jim loves having an Herb Farm, and it's one of the nicest ones you could imagine: large gardens with over three hundred varieties of herbs, a charming shop he built that includes a little bell tower and balcony, vistas to die for in every direction. But listen to Jim:

"If I had to deal with the public every day here, I would be a very unpleasant person. And I don't want to be that. I grew up in a small town grocery store. I know just what it's like with the public at your doorstep seven days a week. I really do love people, but I also love my privacy. This is the way I keep those in balance."

So how does he earn his living on an Herb Farm that only opens regularly one day a week? Long Creek Herb Farm is the center of an extended herbal network Jim has developed over the years. He writes, lectures, develops and sells herbal products, consults around the country on herbs and gardens, and leads a very full and interesting life from an Herb Farm that has become his springboard to the life he enjoys.

Besides the Wednesday visits, Jim responds to requests for special garden tours. *"With herb uses, folklore and herbal history, Jim Long will provide your group (4-8 people) a special tour and lecture, along with herbal drinks and refreshments. Costs average $12*

Jim Long's Long Creek Herb Farm in the Ozarks

per person, with advance reservation. Call for availability. Larger groups (8-12) can request special programs or workshops." This simple announcement in his brochure brings him many requests for special visits to his farm; visits for pre-arranged times and purposes that he can easily schedule.

The farm itself is located between two well visited areas: Eureka Springs in Arkansas, and Branson, Missouri, the newest addition to America's country music Hot Spots. The farm is located in Missouri, but Jim gets his mail in Arkansas, a few miles away. And he has very strong ties to Arkansas that go back to his first visit to Eureka Springs at five years old. "I fell so in love with that place as a child, that I've spent the rest of my life trying to get back and closer to it." Anyone who has ever visited that tiny "Swiss town of the Ozarks" can well imagine how five-year-olds (just as 50-year-olds) are taken with it.

Jim Long's ties to the Ozark Folk Center in Mountain View, Arkansas, have also helped him build his network of varied herb, historical, and business interests. He is a student of American history, especially of the Civil War and the Ozark region, with a strong knowledge and background in the food and medicine plants of that era and area. This reputation of self-taught expertise brought the Ozark Folk Center developers to Jim several years ago to ask that he design the herb gardens at this large, now famous cultural visitor center in Mountain View.

The Center gives herb demonstrations, herb sales, herb dinners, herb festivals—a constant promotion of the plants that many people of the area have known all their lives, and that have now become so popular all over the country. Jim credits Bill and Hillary Clinton with some of the popular herb renaissance in the Ozarks. Hillary Clinton was there for the garden dedication at Mountain View, and both Clintons have been strong promoters of Ozark products, lore, and people.

In our winter visit to Long Creek Herb Farm, Jim was busy answering calls from reporters around the country with questions about the coming Clinton inaugural. What would be served, they wondered? Were there any new or unusual herbs special to the Ozarks that readers around the country would want to know about? Jim takes it easily in stride, talking to any and all callers about the popularity in area kitchens of Mexican mint marigold, lemon basil, lemon verbena, and lemon grass.

Jim grows herbs for only one restaurant, but it happens to be one of the best known restaurants in the region, Dairy Hollow House, whose owner (and children's book writer) Crescent Dragonwagon, would soon join Jim in the nation's capital as Arkansas hosts for the inauguration

For those who would sell fresh culinary herbs to fancy restaurant chefs, Long offers his own experience as helpful guidance:

1. He offers lots of variety: six kinds of basil, three thymes, and four types of shallots. He grows and offers many lemony herbs: lemon verbena, lemon balm, lime thyme, and lemon grass.

2. He charges $1.25 per bunch which consists of 13 sprigs of any herb. Chives and thymes he sells in one inch diameter bunches.

3. With his order he includes a computer list of "What's in the Fridge This Week." This lets all the chefs know what's available, and the herbs won't get lost and buried in complex, fast-working kitchens. It cuts down on their waste.

4. He sometimes makes suggestions with the list: leftover herbs can be used for jelly making; chocolate mint leaves can be candied for after dinner mints. He adds new herbs as they become available in his garden, and tries to keep his own suggestions light in tone and easily readable: This *"horsetail is too coarse to eat, with no real flavor and would probably grind your teeth off, but try short sections as miniature flower holders and stuff them with edible flowers and herbs."* They took his suggestion to heart, says Jim, "and I kept up a continuous harvest of my rampant horsetail all summer for their vases."

Over the years, Jim has reached out to areas all around the country so that his calendar is crowded now with lectures and workshops at herbal events all over the land. Actually, Jim was one of the first people in the country to put on a modern herb festival at his own farm years ago.

He knew lots of herb people and decided they needed to get to know each other. He asked several to be speakers, worked out a menu, sent out invitations at $15 each and, much to his surprise, 50 people showed up and had a wonderful day of herbs. The event grew over the years as he added booths, put up tents, brought in music, raised the prices, and still more people came. Last year 135 people came at $35 dollars each, and Jim decided to call a halt. Seven years was long enough, he said. Let some other people do it, and I'll attend theirs. And he does attend lots of herb fairs and festivals, usually as guest lecturer or workshop leader, sometimes as a consultant helping others with their Herb Farms and events.

Herb products are one of Jim's other specialities: Bread Herb Packets, Bug Repelling Herbal Soap, Fish-Broil Herbs, Moth Repelling Herb Blend, Herbal Bath Blends, Dream Pillow Kits, the list goes on and on. Jim loves to research and develop these products, test them with his own customers, and then wholesale them to other shops around the country. He also carries some of them with him as he goes around the country giving lectures on "Herbal Medicines of the Civil War," "Edible Plants of the Fields and Forest," "History and Lore of Folk Medicines," "Folk Remedies and Herbal Medicines of the Past." He gives demonstrations and workshops on such topics as: "Herbs in the Kitchen," "Preparing Garden Medicinals," "Dream Pillows and Aphrodisiacs," among others. He charges about $200 for an hour's program, and asks that he be reimbursed for travel and lodging expenses. But he welcomes stays in private homes. Herb Farms and Herb Associations around the country rely on his good humored, intelligent presentations to bring them new members and customers. He also teaches at Elderhostel programs in the Ozarks area. He is also a good writer and sells his own booklets on herbs and the making of herbal products.

But always, he returns to the Long Creek Farm, the very center of his life and business. Instead of being tied down to the farm, he uses the farm as his springboard to life. Last year he took on a regular column with *Herb Companion* magazine, and writes a column for the *Ozarks Mountaineer*, plus a syndicated newspaper column on Ozarks Gardening. Almost everything he writes about, he learns in the gardens of his farm. "I'm here," he says, "for the same reason my guests and visitors come here. Because I need to constantly reconnect to the land. This sound of animals around you now, these views in the area, those are all well worn paths in my subconscious—in all our systems. We all have this need to connect to our roots which lie in this ground beneath us."

Does he often get calls to open up on other days? "Oh, yes, all the time. And many times I do. But always fitted in to my schedule so I can get other work done." Right now he has one very part time young woman working occasionally who is anxious to learn about herb businesses and is proving herself a real asset to Jim. "I hadn't realized how far behind I had gotten, until she came along and started doing so much."

When he decided to hire help he also applied for a Missouri Heritage Apprentice Sponsorship, which are usually given, Jim says, for the study of music or crafts. He didn't succeed in the grant application, but after thinking about it that much, he decided he needed to go ahead and take on a part-time employee anyway. "Too often," he remembers, "I'd go somewhere to speak and not have any product to take along simply because I'd run out of time. This herbal renaissance," he says, "is causing every one of us to look again at our businesses and make some tough decisions. Do we really want to get larger, hire help, change the way we've been doing business for years? I know I have to make intentional choices to control the size of my business in order to maintain the enjoyment I have for it."

In advising other small herbal business people, Jim suggests they take advantage of the printing services of the 24 hour a day print shops that have recently sprung up around the country. "I drive over seventy miles to visit a Kinko's shop," he says "because I can sit there and use their computer, ask their help, and design these labels and have them made for about two cents each, or less. It's great for trying new stuff when you aren't sure yet that you are really going ahead on something. I can also make my little booklets there. Day or night. At very low prices."

"And never be afraid to charge a fee," he advises those who want to start teaching about herbs. "If people want a speaker they need to make a commitment. It doesn't have to be a large fee. But a fee will make everyone do a better job." After all, he adds, "they want your time and experience—both things of value."

His other firm advice to those who would start any herbal business:

- Read everything you can about herbs.

- Join your local herb association if one is available.

- If at all possible, attend an International Herb Growers and Marketers Association conference where you can gain a "great perspective to your own direction, and meet others who may already be doing what you plan to do and can save you from mistakes."

- Explore the markets in your area very thoroughly before you decide on any products you wish to offer.

The reference section following these chapters on Herb Farms deals with many of Jim's recommendations.

Jim has an easy, relaxed manner that comes, I think, from a great sense of inner confidence that puts him at ease in any situation. *Gourmet Magazine* did an article recently about Arkansas and gave fine coverage to Dairy Hollow House, where Jim sells most of his fresh herbs. The magazine staff also decided to pay Long Creek Herb Farm a visit as one of the suppliers to the well known restaurant. Jim invited them all to lunch! and had a great time.

"What did you serve?" I wondered, immediately feeling the terror of such an event ever happening to me.

"Well, it was morel season," said Jim, "so that made it easy."

Gourmet Magazine thought it was all fine, too, describing the meal in great detail: "...giant white morels...each as long as my hand," a salad that "tasted the way a spring shower smells," and on and on with a final wink at the reader: "Jim Long declared that he wasn't a cook, just a believer in the culinary powers of herbs."

For months afterward, Jim's phone rang with people wanting to come to lunch. He logged in 154 phone calls and 100 letters from readers anxious to come and enjoy just as the magazine staff had enjoyed. "Great publicity," laughs Jim, "but didn't earn me a dime.

"Orville Redenbacher was no doubt right," he adds. "A person probably ought to do just one thing and do it very well. I feel certain that would be the best advice for my business. But not for my life." And life, after all, is what Jim Long is here for—and knows very well how to live.

Herb Farm Visiting

BEFORE LEAVING THE subject of Herb Farms, I'd like to encourage readers to consider purchasing one of three herb business directories listed in the reference section that follows. If you
are new to the world of herbs, you may not realize just how many
of these lovely spots exist, probably even in your own region. The
directories make it easy to find almost any herb business of any
kind in your area, and I can't stress too much the importance of
reaching out and finding out what's already going on in your own
area as you consider herb business possibilities. The directories
list addresses, telephone numbers, and what the business is
about. They make Herb Farm visiting an easy pleasure.

Secondly, I'd also like to encourage herb enthusiasts to try and
make a visit to the Ozark Folk Center in Mountain View, Arkansas, where Jim Long put in the wonderful herb gardens, and
where herbs are still honored as a part of the culture.

Also, if you travel to New Hampshire or Maine, do try and
get to one of the existing Shaker Villages, where commercial
herb business really began in this country. First their seeds and
herbs, and then their farming equipment, came to be considered
the finest in the country. They were magnificent gardeners and
used herbs in so many ways. We have stayed at the village in
Enfield, New Hampshire, where there are large herb gardens and
a fine museum, and also visited the Sabbathday Shaker Village
in Poland Springs, Maine, where a tiny shop still sells little tins
of herbs and bottles of rose water, just as the Shakers sold them
nearly 200 years ago. If you love herbs (or history), I can guarantee that you will enjoy a visit to one of the Shaker enclaves. I
also recommend a fine book on this subject in the reference section that follows.

Herb Farm References

SUPPLIES

Avatar's World, 9106 Hurd Road, Edgerton, WI 53534. 608-884-4730. FAX 608 884-6920.

Large wholesale supplier of dried materials including ornamental grains and grasses.

Barker Enterprises, 15106 10th Ave. SW, Seattle, WA 98166. 206-244-1870.

Candle making supplies. Catalog $2, refundable with first purchase.

Caswell-Massey, 100 Enterprise Place, Dover, DE 19901. For catalogs, call 800-326-0500. FAX 800-676-3299. Offices, 201-225-2181.

Frontier Cooperative Herbs, 3021 78th St., Norway, IA 52318. 319-227-7996. 800-669-3275 for orders. FAX 319-227-7966.

One of the largest wholesalers of herbs, spices, craft items, oils, etc. Catalog free.

Poly Bags Plus Inc. 3602 Harbor Blvd, Port Charlotte, FL 33952.

Will sell small quantities of muslin, poly and cellophane bags. Free catalog.

Star West, 11253 Trade Center Dr., Rancho Cordova, CA 95742. 916-638-8100. To order, 800-800-HERB (4372).

Bulk supplies of dried herbs, etc.

The Whole Herb Company, PO Box 1203, Sonoma, CA 95476. 707-935-1077. FAX 707-935-3447.

Bulk supplies of dried herbs and spices, oils and teas, potpourri supplies.

Val's Naturals, PO Box 832, Kathleen, FL 33849. 813 858-8991.

Wholesale supplier of dried materials. Free catalog.

See **the reference section on Herbal Products** section for more on supplies.

PUBLICATIONS

Potpourri from Herbal Acres. Quarterly newsletter from Pine Row Publications, Box 428LS, Washington Crossing, PA 18977. $20 per year.

An amazing network publication between Phyllis Shaudys, well known herbal author (see below), and what appears to be all the herb crafters of the nation. Every issue is full of ideas, recipes, herb events across the country, and that irresistible Shaudys enthusiasm for herbs, herbs, herbs.

Herb Gatherings. $15 for 6 issues from 10949 East 200 South, Lafayette, IN 47905.

A recent herb consumer newsletter, with emphasis on issues like indoor herb growing, herb recipes, crafts and some traditional herb medicine lore. Nice graphics.

The Flora-Line. Quarterly newsletter from Berry Hill Press, 7336 Berry Hill, Palos Verdes, CA 90274. $15.

A dried flower emphasis, strong on design and marketing ideas. Sample copy, $3.95

Empire Herb Trail. A Guide to the Herbal Enterprises and Public Herb Gardens in New York State. Available free from Box 640, Trumansburg, NY 14886.

A perfect example of what cooperating herb businesses in an area can put together for their mutual benefit.

HERB BUSINESS DIRECTORIES

Herbal Green Pages. $20 postpaid from *The Herbal Connection*, PO Box 245, Silver Spring, PA 17575.

Over 200 pages of Herb Farms and other herb businesses across the country. Revised every two years. Excellent resource.

Herb Resource Directory. $12.95 postpaid, from Northwind Farm Publications. Rt 2 Box 246, Shevlin, MN 56676.

Hundreds of descriptive listings of Herb Farms and other herb related businesses throughout the country. Published by the folks from *The Business of Herbs.*

Herb Companion Wishbook and Resource Guide. $16.95 plus p&h from Interweave Press, 201 East Fourth St., Loveland, CO 80537.

The emphasis is on mail order herbal resources, but the descriptions let you know if they are open for retail business. Published by *Herb Companion Magazine.*

HERB ASSOCIATIONS

If you should plan to open an Herb Farm (or any other herb business), one of the very first things to do is to reach out and find other herb businesses and enthusiasts in your area. Herb people are the friendliest, most supportive people you can imagine. Here are some of the regional herb associations. If your area isn't covered, check with the people at the Business of Herbs, the International Herb Growers and Marketers Association (IHGMA), or the Herbal Green Pages, the three primary herb networks. Those addresses are in the reference section following the Herb Growing chapters of the book, or listed above in the publications section.

Adirondack Herb Society, Rt 2, Chateaugay, NY 12920.

Andover Herb Society, 17 Boardman Lane, Hamilton, MA 01936.

Arizona Herb Association, PO Box 63101, Phoenix, AZ 85082.

Capital Area Herbal Network, Washington DC, Joe Pye & Friends 703-644-5627.

Central Texas Herb Society, 307 W. Ave. E, Lampassas, TX 76550.

Ginseng Growers Assoc. of Canada, Box 87, Waterford, ON N0E 1Y0, Canada.

Great Northern Botanical Association, PO Box 362, Helena, MT 59701.

Illinois Ginseng Growers Assoc., Rt 2, Box 261, Pittsfield, IL 62363. 217-285-6022.

Illinois Herb Association, c/o Illinois Specialty Growers Association, 1701 Towanda Ave, Bloomington, IL 61701. 309-557-2107.

Inland Herb Society, PO Box 8657, Riverside, CA 92515.

Kentucky Herb Growers Association, PO Box 182, Washington, KY 41096.

Maryland Herb Association, PO Box 388, Millington, MD 21651.

Michigan Herb Business Association, 2540 North Setterbo Road, Suttons Bay, MI 49682.

North Carolina Herb Association, Rt 1 Box 65, Godwin, NC 28344.

Northeast Herb Association, PO Box 146, Marshfield, VT 05658.

Oklahoma Herb Growers Association, 2087 E. 71st St., Ste. 114, Tulsa, OK 74136.

Ozark Regional Herb Growers & Marketers Assoc., Rt 3 Box 3500, Theodosia, MO 65761.

Pennsylvania Herb Business Association, 717-697-5111.

Smokey Mountain Herb Society, 1743 W. Broadway, Ste. 172, Maryville, TN 37801.

Texas Herb Growers & Marketers Association, Rt 8, Box 567, Brownsville, TX 78520.

Virginia Herb Growers and Marketers Assoc., PO Box 1176, Chesterfield, VA 23832.

West Virginia Herb Association, Rt 1, Box 263, Weston, WV 26452.

Herb Society of America, Inc., 9019 Kirtland-Chardon Road, Mentor, OH 44060. 216-256-0514.

A membership group, "not medically oriented," formed in 1933 for the purpose of "furthering the knowledge and use of herbs..." They sponsor research and tours, help establish public herb gardens, review lots of herb books, and offer lots of information on herbs. Membership is by recommendation or sponsorship.

OTHER RESOURCES TO CONSIDER

For basic business and tax information, be sure to look into the offerings at your **local community college.** In our community, they put on at least one, sometimes two, series a year of relatively short classes on business taxes, business bookkeeping, fund raising, etc. Practical, helpful, and inexpensive.

Ozark Folk Center, PO Box 500, Mountain View, AR 72560. 501-269-3851. 800-264-FOLK.

You can call or write and get on their mailing list for notices of their seminars, workshops, herbal feasts, and musical events. They also have a lodge adjoining.

United Society of Shakers, Rt 1, Box 640, Poland Spring, ME 04274. Museum, gardens and Shaker Store are open Memorial Day through Columbus Day.

Their tins of herbs and teas are available through mail order. A tour of their property is fascinating. America's original herbalists are certainly worth knowing—or at least knowing about.

Lower Shaker Village, Route 4A, Enfield, New Hampshire 03748. 603-632-4346.

A rather large historical site with many original Shaker buildings, beautiful herb gardens, plus a renowned Shaker Museum. The Shaker Inn and Restaurant, now privately owned, operates in the impressive old Great Stone Dwelling. Classes and workshops are offered. Contact them for a schedule.

HERB FARM BUSINESSES

Windbeam Herb Garden. Peter & Nanette Cimino, 1106 Stagecoach Rd., Stowe, VT 05672

Silver Bay Herb Farm. Mary Preus, 9151 Tracyton Blvd., Bremerton, WA 98310

Meadowsweet Farm. Polly & Elliott Haynes, 729 Mt. Holly Rd., North Shrewsbury, VT 05738

Summers Past Farms. Sheryl & Marshall Lozier, 15602 Olde Highway 80, Flinn Springs, CA 92021

Long Creek Herb Farm. Jim Long, Rt 4, Box 730, Oak Grove, AR 72660

RECOMMENDED BOOKS

The Book of Potpourri, by Penny Black. Simon and Schuster, New York, 1989.

Written by an English gardener whose products are sold world-wide. Potpourri makers like to keep their own recipes to themselves, but here is a book that in both text and pictures can give anyone a running start on making wonderful scented mixtures. Basic recipes for potpourri plus added special touches, and with many inspiring ways to display and present the mixes.

The Earth Shall Blossom: Shaker Herbs and Gardening, by Galen Beale and Mary Rose Boswell. Countryman Press, Vermont, 1991.

A splendid book for putting at least a little of the solid base of the early Shaker herb business experience under our own present endeavors. They made seed and herb businesses both reputable and profitable, and their story is fascinating. Yes, they were seen to "shake" as they danced, but it's everything else they did that's still so impressive.

Everlasting Flowers For Pleasure & Profit, by Jeannette Verhelst. PO Box 178, Radville, Sask., S0C 2G0, Canada, 1991.

One of the few books on dried flowers with suggestions and coverage of some of the business potential of dried flowers.

Gifts & Crafts From The Garden, by Maggie Oster. Rodale Press, Pennsylvania, 1988.

Here is a good basic craft book to set the hands to work in dealing with material from the garden. It begins with dried flower and herb arrangements, their application on hats, lamp shades, baskets, wall hangings and wreaths; crafts from pressed flowers; sachets, pillows, incense making, vinegars and simple beauty care products, basket making, and wheat weaving. In other words, all the things you might want to make and/or sell if you had an Herb Farm with a little retail outlet. Simple, user-friendly instructions, line drawn details and some colored photos.

The Pleasure of Herbs, by Phyllis Shaudys. Storey Publications, Vermont, 1986.

Everyone's favorite introductory book to herbs. Enthusiasm on every page. An almost insistent sharing style that would overcome even the most hesitant herb beginner. Ranges from what to put in an herbal footbath to how to start an herbal sachet business at home, from how to seal and decorate herbal vinegar bottles, to ideas for giving an herbal wedding.

Growing a Business, by Paul Hawken. Simon & Schuster, New York, 1987.

I didn't get around to reading this until my own book was nearly finished. Now I wish I had read this inspiring little book when I first heard about it, which was years ago. If you are thinking about a business of any kind, read this book. Hawken makes you see that running a good little business can be the best of occupations, can bring out your undeveloped talents, can be good for your community and even for the world. And that " ...your best idea for a business will be something that is deep within you, something that can't be stolen because it is uniquely yours.... The idea itself is just the tip of the iceberg. The iceberg is your life." A mighty fine book. It also includes some practical stuff too, like how to think about writing up a business plan.

Homemade Money, by Barbara Brabec. Betterway Publications, Virginia. 1984.

Written by an early, and now leading authority on the booming home-based business phenomenon in America, Brabec's book is a comprehensive look at how to set up and succeed at such a business. Planning, location, employees, zoning, publicity, marketing, etc. Large format. 300 pages.

Small Time Operator, by Bernard Kamoroff CPA. Bell Springs Publishing, Laytonville, CA, 1984.

If you have never run a business before (and maybe even if you have), I would suggest this book as a first. Designed to tell you "how to start your own small business, keep your books, pay your taxes, and stay out of trouble!" It combines a breezy, easily read style with serious, important information. It includes the ledgers and worksheets to last you through your first year. I understand it is also now available on a computer disc. This is one of the most recommended small business books in the country—with good reason.

HERBAL PRODUCTS

Commercial products often come into being

because people make them first of all as gifts

for friends and family, then get lots of

encouragement from the recipients and

decide to go on from there.

Herbal Products

There's a little plant that grows on our island called pipsissewa. Jerry Jameson, the produce manager at our local market, tells me that his grandmother, an early resident here, made tea from that plant. Jerry and I have daydreamed a little about mixing up a batch of tea with pipsissewa and some herbs from my garden. I have a small food dryer; we could try different combinations until we got one that tasted good. Then we could market it in a tiny brown paper bag with a little label attached. Our investment would be minimal, until we could see that it sells well.

We haven't done it yet, but the idea is there, and both of us think that a local, good-tasting tea could sell well, both to locals and to tourists who pour through our town by the thousands in July and August of every year.

My point here is that herbal products can have just such a simple beginning. Herbal soaps, teas, vinegars, potpourri, to name just a few, can often be done in your home to begin with, keeping your investment low while you test the market for the product. Commercial products often come into being because people make them first of all as gifts for friends and family, then get lots of encouragement from the recipients and decide to go on from there.

This kind of early stage development is incredibly valuable because you learn each step so thoroughly, know what it is you can expect the product to do and, most importantly, what it is your customer wants and will buy. Once you are past the gift giving stage of something you are developing, the next usual step is to market it either in a shop or at a farmers' or craft market. The farmers' market step can be ever so valuable, too, because of the face to face encounter with your customers.

I'll never forget the sudden and dramatic knowledge I gained from just such an encounter years ago when I took my little pots of herbs and homemade herb jellies to the famous Pike Place Market in Seattle. I had sold them easily here in Friday Harbor to friends and neighbors, even to tourists. Then I decided to try the big city market. If you've ever been to the Pike Place Market you know what I mean by an army of customers moving down those aisles. It was amazing. After a few times at the market, I began to relax a little and to notice things more from the customer's point of view. I'd lean out and look way down the aisles to notice all these people moving towards my table, all tasting, touching, smelling, smiling and nodding at the growers and craftsmen, and I realized how they were educating themselves as consumers. They had almost everything anyone could ever imagine laid out before them in a colorful, tasty, nearly overwhelming display of choices, and really, I thought, they were just waiting for someone to bowl them over with something they thought for the moment they couldn't live without. There wasn't any sign of need or want showing on any faces that I could see, except for the street people outside the aisles in the streets, and even they looked somewhat jaded, and I suddenly felt a depressing insight into this passion we have for buying and selling: the American consumer **adores** shopping, but he really doesn't **need** anything. He's training himself almost daily to recognize better and better quality, yet his real needs are fewer and fewer.

Not a very cheery thought for would-be product developers, I know, but the point I'd like to get across is that, even though I think it's relatively easy to start and sell a product in your local area, when you decide to try and put that product into the larger (vs. local) market, it pays to remember that it is a very tough, competitive market out there and that you need to be ready to get quite serious about your investment and effort. The American consumer now has much, much more to choose from than she can ever use; she's growing more sophisticated in her tastes and, at the very same time, the economy may be on a long winding road of slow growth. I keep those thoughts ever in the back of my mind when I think about marketing products.

In the front of my mind is the awareness of the amazing changes taking place both in the minds of consumers and in the marketplace, and the certainty I feel that herbs and herbal products are going to continue to grow ever more popular with American consumers. For now these products are still very much a part of the edge or fringe of the market, but they are beginning to move towards the center. We've probably all seen the TV ads for Tom's of Maine® toothpastes, and Kwai® garlic—herbal products that have already moved into the very center of our mass market. I know that movement will continue as many of us grow more and more aware of our health and healthy products, and turn more away from synthetic or over-produced food and products. The education of the American consumer seems to be moving into fast forward, and herbal products are going to be very much in demand.

What follows are some case histories, if you will, of herbalists who make and market herbal products. Their products and experience will not likely be yours, but you can learn from them, fit some of their story around your own and, hopefully, ease your own path during the process of developing and marketing your own herbal products, if that should be your interest. The reference section following these chapters will give you more specific information on resources, herbal product associations, etc.

Dona Flora, La Conner, Washington

BETH HAILEY, WHO owns and operates Dona Flora Herbs and Flowers, is by no means a novice at her business, but she well remembers the beginnings of it. Now, as she is poised to try to send one or two of her products into a much wider market, she took time to talk with me about the beginnings of her company and about some ideas new herb business people might want to think about as they consider their own start-ups. A little reality check-up, we might call this.

Beth began where most successful herb business people begin—with a passion for herbs that started when she was very young. Her first business efforts were in selling her own fresh flowers and fresh cut herbs to a local up-scale restaurant in the town of La Conner, where she happened to be working. She also worked as a volunteer at that time for the regional food co-op, and was soon selling her fresh herbs through the co-op. That retail store experience, even as a volunteer, has been especially helpful in her own business education.

Beth has now been growing, selling, and working with herbs for over 12 years and stresses the importance of working in your local community first, where you can get lots of feedback and make certain you are developing something that is both useful and wanted. It is through this local outreach that many herbal products get their start: first to friends and neighbors, and then to craft shows and farmers' markets—always making any necessary changes in recipes, product names, or in price. Finally, when you feel comfortable with your product and have gotten lots of positive feedback from those who use it, it may be time to try for that larger market.

The Dona Flora product line today includes body care products such as gardener's salve, foot cream, facial steams, and bathing herbs; plus Dona Flora Edibles, including teas, vinegars, herb blends, and spiced oils. Several of the products come in different sizes; all have handsome labels and are shown in a good looking brochure with both a retail and a wholesale price list.

Like most beginners, Beth didn't pay a lot of attention to her labels and packaging when she first started: the product itself was the most important thing. Then, a talented friend designed a lovely logo for her, and a talented sister-in-law de-

Dona Flora's packaging features this lovely logo

signed a new label. Dona Flora sales went up immediately, and markedly.

The vinegars were the food products that Beth marketed first, showing and selling them at local fairs and a farmers' market. She now produces twenty varieties that she retails at $4.65 for a twelve ounce bottle. It was while she was working on the vinegars that she first started thinking seriously about the process and costs of manufacturing. At that time she made up a very careful pricing formula that she has used ever since and that she now applies to each product she develops.

"Most people tend to underprice their products to begin with," she says, remembering that she did that too, in the beginning. Beth decided early on to discipline herself to a pricing formula so as to keep from losing money in the confusion of bringing out a product and putting it into competition. It is so easy in these early phases to concentrate only on the selling (do the customers like it? will they buy it?) and lose track of the importance of the bottom line (can I afford to make and sell this?)

If you are making your very first efforts at selling something you create, say at an annual craft show in your community, you may not yet be really interested in the bottom line. Perhaps you just want to see how your goods stack up with others, to see if you like being out there in the commercial world, face to face with people who can say yes or no to what you make. In that case, you probably just want to look around and see what others charge for something similar and fit yourself into the picture.

This casual, almost hobby method of creating and selling goes on all the time at farmers' markets and craft shows, and, incidentally, drives regular sellers who are trying to make a living on their products a little crazy. Regular craft market sellers feel like they have to compete constantly with people who are there on a lark and don't really need the money or the business. But if you are at all serious about learning to sell what you make, and learning to make a profit on it, Beth's pricing formula can be especially helpful to you. Importantly, her method **includes a charge for her own labor** in the formula—something hobby or beginning sellers usually leave out.

She makes up her pricing formula on an 8½"x11" form that she uses to price everything. The product ingredients are listed down the left side of the page, along with their current prices. In the first column to the right, she lists the date of the price, as ingredient prices change quite often. In the next column she lists the cost of the ingredient including the shipping. Then comes a column she calls the *formula to extend*, which gives the price per pound (or ounce) of the ingredient multiplied by the amount of the ingredient used in the batch she is making. The final column, on the right, gives the dollar per batch price: just how

EXAMPLE				
INGREDIENT	DATE	PRICE/ AMOUNT	FORMULA TO EXTEND	COST FOR THIS BATCH
Fragrant Oil	3/94	$49.50 / 1/2gal	3 oz x $1.55/oz	$4.64

much she is spending on this ingredient to make the whole batch.

She continues down the page listing every ingredient that goes into the product. For her own fresh herbs that she grows and uses in the products, she adds a cost of $10 a pound, fresh, or whatever she knows she would have to pay to replace those herbs. She adds up the cost of the ingredients and to this total she then adds the cost of her labor to make this whole batch. She figures her labor at a moderate price per hour, but well above the minimum wage. She then physically divides the batch by pouring it into the different sized jars, adds the cost of the jars and the cost of the labels, which also includes the labeling labor cost, and comes up with a fairly true cost for material and labor.

This is probably as far as most hobby sellers ever tend to get in their pricing. They feel they've covered their costs and, wow, even allowed themselves say, eight or ten dollars per hour for labor costs. Maybe they were just having fun anyway, and finding out if their efforts would sell. That's fine. But if you are at all serious about putting a product into the marketplace beyond your local craft show or farmers' market, then just allowing yourself a labor charge is not enough to cover the true costs of your business. The minute you hire even one part time employee, you can be in the hole.

It's also time to remember the parts that newcomers tend to forget about entirely: taxes and overhead. If you are making products at home, whether legally or not, you should think about that as only a temporary situation. You may need to move into a properly zoned, probably inspected and rented building one of these days. Your product should reflect that as soon as it goes into the larger marketplace, so that you don't have to keep raising your prices because you failed to take any of these things into consideration. Now, what about equipment? Perhaps you can continue to use your own kitchen equipment for the time being, but if you are making a food product, that would not be acceptable to the state or county inspectors. And equipment, of course, wears out, and needs repairing or replacing.

Now, what about taxes? First of all, in our state there is a business tax (although no state income tax) and there are the employee taxes. The rules and laws are very strict on these taxes, and the costs are not inconsiderable. What about property taxes, if you can have a manufacturing facility on your own property? And telephone costs, and costs for printing, and all those other costs to let the world know your product is available? And delivery charges? And the cost of any money you might have borrowed to do all this? And the bank charges, if you accept credit card purchases? The list goes on and on.

So, after the cost of ingredients and direct labor cost, Beth (like other manufacturers) adds on enough to try and cover all these costs and to allow for some profit and company growth. Beth's method is to almost (but not quite) **double the ingredients + basic labor cost**. This price becomes her wholesale price and the one she calls her *bottom line.* "I know that if I go much below this bottom line that I could risk losing money. If I can stay above it, I'll be OK."

Others mark up more, or less, depending on how they view all of these other charges and, importantly, how it will affect the retail price. Some crafters use a rule of thumb that takes the direct cost of materials, including packaging (but not the labor), and marking that up five times to cover everything else. Others use other formulas, and the reference section following these chapters will recommend books about this subject. When I talked to Beth about the formula of five, she tried it on her calculator with a couple of her own products and found that it resulted in figures very close to her own. But she trusts her own pricing formula, and comparing that to a different one only confirmed that she's on the right track.

Admittedly, this is a lot to think about as you are labeling up your first bottles of vinegar or your first bars of soap to try and sell to a local gift shop. And, of course, there's even more to it than this. Each time you reach out to sell to a wider circle, you have to remember about those who will be doing your selling to the final retail customer, and be aware of what they will be charging. In most instances, the wholesale cost of a product, like the ones we are talking about, will be doubled at the retail level to cover the retailer's costs of keeping her doors open and making a profit herself. It's important to always keep that eventual retail cost in mind, so that you don't price yourself out of the market. It also helps to keep a close eye on the retail prices of many other products like yours, and to be sure that the quality of your product always supports the retail price of it.

You cannot determine the exact retail price of your product, but you should expect up to a 100 per cent markup, or a doubling of the wholesale price you get for your product. If you sell to basic grocery stores, they operate on a lower markup on many items than do the specialty shops, but grocery stores, too, are always looking to make a higher markup, if possible.

You may be able to sell quite a few bottles of vinegar, or bars of soap, or packets of potpourri in your local area, and that may be enough to satisfy your business ambitions. Many people choose to stop at this level and are content to become a high quality community resource, and to do enough business that way to make their efforts very worthwhile. That is certainly true with many small growers. But once you think about a much wider circle for sales, there are still other costs that must be taken into account.

Showing your products at large regional or national craft or gift shows can be quite expensive and even require several overnight hotel stays; the display booth fees are usually high; extra brochures and product information are necessary. Or perhaps you would want to get sales people to represent your product on their own selling routes. That means paying some of their expenses and their commissions, plus other added costs.

Truly national distribution of a product almost always requires dealing with brokers or distributors, those middlemen of commerce who, for a fee, will warehouse your product along with a zillion others, and list it in their big catalogs and deliver it to all the stores who can't be bothered dealing with countless small product manufacturers like yourself. When you decide to try to distribute your product across the nation, or even to a section of it out of your immediate reach, the product has to have enough profit margin in it to allow this middle broker or distributor to also make a small profit.

This much larger picture is beyond the scope of this book and leads to other subjects like contract production and bottling for much larger quantities. But I do think it's important for even beginners to be at least a little bit aware of this larger picture as they start finding their own place in the market, and I do list some references that go into detail about this kind of marketing.

Right now the Dona Flora food and cosmetic products are manufactured by Beth in a local rented commercial kitchen for which she pays an hourly fee as rent. She grows herbs and flowers both at home and on land she leases nearby. Beth has one part-time employee through much of the year and up to six part-time employees during the flower harvest season. She dries her flowers in a large barn on her own property, near her home and greenhouse.

A determined environmentalist, Beth thinks small businesses are good for the world but worries that herbs and herbal businesses are becoming a very trendy thing with too many small operators getting into them and thus bringing both quality and price down for everyone. "I worry that too many people think this would be such a simple way to make money. And it isn't. It's lots of hard work. And not a really big return. At least not yet."

Beth is closely tied in to her community through the co-op and often brings out or tries a new product in direct response to the needs of particular customers: simpler salves, for instances, for those with skin sensitivities. One of her products, Skagit Salve, is named for the wide river valley that is home to her and her community. Her brochure also offers to do *custom formulating of our body care and edible products.*

"If someone comes to me wanting a massage oil with walnut and olive oil and herbs," says Beth, "I can do that blend for them. If they like it, I figure out a cost for them. Then, if I think it has possibilities beyond one customer, I look into packaging, labels, and so forth. Also," she adds, "I've done several tea blends for stores who want their own blend."

Beth is cutting back on the dried flowers after many years of growing and marketing them, and beginning now to concentrate a little more on putting her gardener's salve into a larger market. Competition in the dried flower market, she says, is now too great from the large growers, and too plentiful from home gardeners bringing small crops to market in every farmers' market.

Beth, like other salve makers, began by working with recipes for small amounts of salve to be made at home. Many herb books contain these simple recipes. That beginning gave her the *sense* of the product and something to build on. Nowadays, she keeps her recipe secret, but does stress that temperature tending is a tricky part of the procedure, so as not to ruin the properties of the salve ingredients by using too much heat.

She still uses basic kitchen equipment and sets everything up ahead of time to make the operation go smoothly and without error. She keeps her working and pouring utensils on clean trays so that any spills can be saved. When it's ready, she pours the mixture into the different sized jars, waits for the salve to set up, adds the lids, then the labels, and puts everything into boxes ready for shipping.

Whenever she sells the gardener's salve at farmers' markets, she charges the following prices: ¼ oz @ $2.50; 1½ oz @ $4.25; 6 oz @ $9.25; 16 oz @$23. Her wholesale prices for those sizes are $1.50; $2.53; $6.15, and $14.55.

Four years ago Beth got a call from a London company asking if she could deliver 900 jars of the gardener's salve within the following three weeks. The order came in the middle of the flower season and was by far her largest single order ever. She agreed to it after asking for an extra week for the processing. That company remained one of her very best accounts until recently when, sadly, it succumbed to the long downturn in the British economy and went out of business.

The long local success with the salve, and her ability to keep up with the orders from at least one large company, makes Beth realize now that she can, and should, try to contact many potential new customers. The increasing market in mail order shopping is her likely target, and a large American mail order firm, specializing in garden merchandise, has already found the salve on their own and written to her recently for prices and samples. She senses it is time to make a push.

Beth will only work on pushing this one product first, because it has been well tested in the marketplace, she has already learned how to make it in fairly large batches, and because she is basically quite conservative and careful in all things financial. She lives comfortably, but frugally; never, ever, borrows money; and is certain that her successes have come because she has learned well, thought a lot about what she is doing, and been patient and careful. Beth was widowed six years ago and, though she still looks much like a college student herself, she now has one youngster away at college and another, now a senior in high school, still at home. She really can't afford to take the chances some can take who have another breadwinner standing by to keep everything from flying apart in the event of a failure. But her own hard efforts have carried the family along so far, and there's every sign that she will continue to succeed.

She recently attended her first herb trade show given by the International Herb Growers and Marketers Association. This last year it was held in Seattle, so Beth could rather easily go and attend the classes and even sell some of her products in the evening herb bazaar. She stresses how important she feels it is for new herb business people to reach out to others working in their own area, especially to anyone who might be a competitor, and to work together so as to enhance rather than hurt or decrease each other's businesses.

The high-schooler comes home, there are a few orders to ship, some seedlings to tend. I go on my way as Beth hands me a little jar of gardener's salve to try. It smells like it's made from the very essence of juicy, tender-stemmed green plants. I rub it on, and it feels like my hands have been wanting this gentle treatment for years. Perfect.

Balsam Fir Products, Maine

WENDY NEWMEYER LEARNED about aromatic balsam fir when she and her husband, Jack, moved in the late '70s to 100 acres of land covered with balsam fir trees. They had worked and saved for years, always looking for land that they both liked and could afford to buy.

They found the land in Maine, moved a little trailer onto it and, with running water that came only from a creek, set about growing their own vegetables and preserving their own food, barely surviving, they remember now, as they took stock and tried to figure out how to earn their way.

High energy, extremely hard work, endless plans for the future, incredibly strong ties to the land, a keen awareness of how the system works—all of these have been turned into a lifestyle with big payoffs for the Newmeyers. When someone mentions modern "back to the landers," I think of Wendy and Jack and their 100 acres in Maine. They searched out every Realtor in the state to find this piece of land. It is full of moose, deer, beaver, raccoons, bear, fox, a year-round stream with otters, and, because it had only small forests, small fields, and small flatlands, no one else was interested. They could buy it for only $16,500.

They read and took seriously the advice of Scott & Helen Nearing, among the most famous of America's rural sages: to give yourself two or three years of income as a cushion in making the transition from city to country, because it could take that long to learn to make your way in a rural or wilderness area.

The Newmeyers tried growing and selling herbs, Christmas trees, vegetables, and cut firewood, while all around them the fragrant trees were being cut for paper and pulp.

Wendy heard that an incense plant in Lewiston would buy the leftover tree tops and boughs cut up into small pieces, and she soon got a contract with the incense plant to bring them cut-up balsam fir boughs for seven cents a pound.

"I just loved going into that plant," she recalls, "because the smell was so powerful and grand." Although primarily an incense manufacturing plant, the Lewiston company also made and sold a very plain balsam pillow, a long tradition in Maine.

"I looked at that pillow week in and week out for ages, every time I went in there to sell my boughs, and thought, *great idea, but why doesn't someone do something with a little more pizzazz?*"

Meanwhile, she noticed an ad in one of the herb magazines advertising balsam for pillow making at $10 per pound. She called the woman to offer her cheaper balsam—Wendy was still being paid seven cents a pound for balsam boughs—and found that the woman had been buying the plain Lewiston pillows, taking them apart and making and selling pillow kits from that.

"Hmmmm, maybe there is something to this aromatic pillow business. I'll think some more about it."

The Newmeyers bought a $700 garden chipper and set about trying to figure out how to shred and dry the balsam fir. Wendy then sent out a mailer, with a tiny sample of dried balsam fir needles, to 300 herb businesses offering to supply balsam at $5 per pound, with the price going down to $2 per pound in quantities of 50 or more pounds. Jack built a small drying room with dehumidifiers where he stacked the screened trays of balsam and found out just how slow it is to dry, how much it wants to stick together, change color, mold, and be just plain difficult to deal with.

Wendy's first mailer brought back an astounding response of orders—nearly 50 per cent, and they were soon on their way to becoming the only national supplier of raw balsam. Today that part of the balsam business is still there, but it represents only about 10 per cent of the Newmeyer business, because, along the way, Wendy finally got around to making some balsam pillows with pizzazz.

Aromatic pillows, dream pillows, herb pillows—all are becoming more and more popular just as herbs and fragrances are becoming more popular. Balsam pillows have a long tradition in the northeast. Wendy has pillows from 70 years ago, still very fragrant, still considered very healthful, especially to clear up congestion or to give relief to those with asthma.

When Wendy started with pillows she had a local tee shirt shop do some Maine wildlife designs on fabric. She then cut out the pillows, sewed up three sides, filled them with balsam, hand stitched them closed, made little hang tags that told about the history of balsam pillows, and took a couple of the designs—a loon and moose—to the Audubon gift shop in Falmouth, Maine. They bought them immediately and helped Wendy realize she had a very saleable product to work with.

Maine gets a million visitors every summer, she thought, so why not try to sell one of these pillows to one out of every thousand of those visitors this year? That would mean doing 10,000 pillows that first spring and summer: designing and selling them, cutting, sewing, shipping, billing, and collecting for them. She increased her samples by adding a bear and a chickadee and set out around the area in her car.

"I drove into one little town after another, looked around carefully as I knew I should only sell to one shop in each town, and tried to pick the perfect shop for the pillows. I'd walk in and, honestly, it was like they were waiting for me. I wrote 10 new accounts a day, every day. I started with an eight-inch pillow that would retail for $10, and some shopkeepers asked for smaller ones that would retail for only $5. So I went home and made some of those, got some local artists to work on new designs and went back out on the road." Wendy and Jack worked from 4 AM to midnight those first couple of years and soon began putting local women to work helping to make pillows.

Once you reach this point with a product business and have to have help in the manufacturing, you must decide whether to move into a factory with employees who come every day and work a shift for an hourly or piece rate, or whether you can operate with workers who work at home, either as your employees or as independent, self-employed contractors. This is a very important consideration, so, before deciding on such a step, **make sure you have learned the state rules where you live**. In California, for instance, home working is forbidden in many crafts, especially work on anything wearable. We learned this lesson the hard way several years ago in our own garment manufacturing company when we allowed a woman, who could no longer come to the factory because of her husband's illness, to do some sewing at home. This ended up costing us dearly in fines and penalties. I urge you to pay strict attention to this and also to the zoning laws where you live. To learn about the labor laws, contact the labor department of your state. To learn about zoning laws, contact your town, city, or county and ask for a copy of the zoning restrictions and a copy of the zoning map. I also recommend several business books that cover some of these issues in more detail in the reference section following these chapters on herbal products, and in the other reference sections of the book.

If you make something at your own home and then take it out to sell you must consider the zoning rules of your own area. There are lots of rules in towns and counties that try to separate living from working or production. Any time you bring employees into your home or do anything commercial on your property, chances are there are many rules that come into play, especially if you happen to live in the suburbs where the residential/commercial demarcations are quite strict. If you live in an urban or rural area, the rules will probably be different and not quite so difficult to work around.

Happily, this once tightly controlled situation is starting to give a little under an economy that is more and more suited for home-based businesses. My opinion has always been that if we all treated our work places as though they were our homes—or if we all worked in and from our homes—we would have far fewer environmental problems. It amazes me that intelligent people fight like mad to preserve recreation areas for their weekends, and let their work areas be overwhelmed with pollution, over-crowding, crime, and chaos.

In Maine, at the time of our visit, Wendy had a dozen women sewing in their homes for her company. In that state, if home workers are provided with materials and given instructions, they are considered employees, so Wendy pays workmen's compensation, Social Security, etc. She started out paying her workers piece rates, but has since moved to an hourly rate. All the pillows are hand finished, which is what is done in the homes. The little pillows are stuffed with balsam needles at the tiny building that suffices for a plant on the Newmeyer property, then stacked in boxes to be picked up and returned finished by the workers. Jack and Wendy are planning a larger facility and would like to have several people sewing at the site so that she could fill orders more completely and not have to deal with partial shipments and ever growing shipping costs. But right now they just don't have the room and must often late ship bits and pieces to complete an order. Every shipment, of course, adds to the cost of the product.

They buy 3000 pounds of balsam boughs every week to shred and dry in the drying room. The stuffing and shipping takes up every additional inch of the building, and the fabric cutting is done with a rotary cutter in the attached studio of the Newmeyer home—a nearby lovely log home that Jack has crafted when not working on the business.

Wendy continues to handle most of the sales and this is another area where her experience can be helpful to anyone. She feels she has avoided credit problems by doing almost all the original selling herself. "I think I'm only attracted to honest people," she laughs, and says her experience using sales representatives has not been good: after trying "25 different ones," she has found only one who really writes quite a few orders. But over the years, through the trade shows and Wendy's traveling, they have built up over 3,000 retail accounts including some in Japan, Canada, France, and Italy. They require a $50 minimum on orders and they do the bulk of their business in orders of about $200 each. They offer credit terms of *net 30*, which means the net amount (with no discounts) is due in 30 days. They write a lot of business at the trade and gift shows, and out of a thousand orders will probably not be paid for about ten, an excellent record in today's up and down economy.

Wendy keeps up an active role in Maine craft groups and shows and offers advice freely to others in her area who are trying to make the transition from retailing at craft shows to wholesaling to a much larger customer base. Although she began Maine Balsam Fir Products in the wholesale arena, she usually recommends that people start with craft shows and learn their own limitations and capacities through that process. "The number one complaint against crafters who wholesale," she tells them, "is that they don't take themselves seriously and they don't ship on time." You can learn a lot of this discipline by working lots of craft shows. And wholesale buyers, she says, check out these shows nationwide, in order to find new products.

Over the years the Newmeyers have won some major accounts such as L.L. Bean and Eddie Bauer, "but those really took a long time," says Wendy, who has learned to never, ever push buyers. "Anytime I've really pushed hard on someone," she recalls, "the account has turned out to be a nightmare." Their product brochures are full-page glossy four-color sheets showing all the designs they offer: Victorian pillows, ethnic designs, and clever old sayings—I Pine For You and Balsam Too. Stores and resorts can also order the pillows with shop or geographic names on them.

Their future is full of new plans and products. The vegetable garden has now been turned into a catnip patch. A couple of years ago they started buying their vegetables from another organic grower, and put in 100 catnip plants where the garden used to be in order to try some catnip items. By the second year they had grossed over $4,000 on the little patch of catnip. Wendy also wants to get into cedar pillows, hop pillows, and other aromatic products, but first they must build a real factory and "get the business out of our living room." Some of their property goes through to State Route 219 where they can someday put in both a factory and a retail gift shop. Wendy has already named it, *The Indian Princess Gift Shop*, because of their own strong interest in Indian lore and artifacts.

In her previous life in New Jersey, Wendy delivered newspaper bundles every day and met Jack, a police officer, when she was only 19 years old. They knew they wanted to leave the city and set about working to save enough to do it. For their first seven years in Maine, they lived in a little trailer without electricity and hauled water from their stream. Now they have a fine home, run a good, environmentally-sound business that salvages boughs from logging operations, and they offer employment to other local area artists and seamstresses.

We want you to know that we're not harming the forest in any way for our business. The balsam we use is salvaged from trees already cut for the logging and paper industries, reads the little card accompanying all orders.

I see the Newmeyer experience as one of people making the very best of what this country has to offer. America really is an opportunity society. As much as I and others would like to think America really stands for lots of other, seemingly more important things, what we actually stand for in the world is a chance for people to start out with very little, work hard and make money. Plenty of it. What's exciting about the Newmeyer story, and maybe about the whole concept I'm thinking about, is that people can take this opportunity and turn it into something that's not only good for them, but also good for their environment and for the other people around them. The Newmeyer land is much as they found it, still full of trees and wildlife, an unpolluted stream still running through it. Their own situation has changed dramatically, but they have not spoiled the land to gain from it. They set a very good example for those who would earn their way on the land.

UniTea Herbs, Colorado

IN THE '70s and '80s, Celestial Seasonings® of Boulder, Colorado, introduced herbal teas onto the shelves of nearly every regional supermarket, and onto the menus of almost every type of restaurant in the country. This proved to be a fine opening of a very wide door for herbal products in America. As the teas gained enormous popularity, many herbal products slipped through that door behind Celestial Seasonings® and found their own special niche, sometimes even in direct contrast to the large tea company that has often taken criticism for its use of non-organic and even irradiated ingredients.

UniTea Herbs, also of Boulder, is one such interesting company that well reflects the kind of new business ethics and practices we found so often in our visits to small herb companies around the country. It is also an example of a company with a very cautious approach to growth and company control—important issues for new and growing businesses.

At the time of our visit, UniTea was just hitting a quarter million dollars in yearly sales, yet the company consisted of only a few people: the owners, Brigitte Mars, and her husband, Tom Pfeiffer, Jack Siddall, the business manager (who also does the shipping), and Wes Heilman, production manager, who blends all the teas using Brigitte's formulas, plus Sunflower, Tom & Brigitte's 22-year-old daughter.

The company has been growing at nearly 15 per cent per year, and has only recently put in a computer system. Siddall has a degree in business which complements his long time serious interest in naturopathic medicine. The business is housed in a small (1000 square feet) building along a popular shopping street in this charming college town. To visitors, the enterprise gives the impression of a very relaxed working environment surrounding an efficient, well designed little business machine that can and will simply run on forever.

The UniTea product is a series of 12 blended medicinal teas sold through grocers, health food and herb shops. The bulk teas are sold retail by weight from large glass jars with incredibly beautiful labels on them; each customer scoops out the amount wanted into a little paper sack and then takes one of the lovely labels home to use on their own tea container. Recently they added a four-ounce, recyclable, plastic jar to use with the labels, and that is refillable wherever their teas are sold. They work and think long and hard to keep down packaging expenses and problems, in order to keep from adding waste to the growing trash streams flowing from our homes and businesses into the land-fills and incinerators around the country.

These teas are not finely ground and milled like tea bag teas, but have a great look to them of real, even recognizable ingredients, that will brew up strong and effective teas. Over-milling, the UniTea people believe, takes the strength from most tea blends. And their blends are a fascinating mix of American, Chinese, and European herbs blended to make delicious aromatic beverages with appealing names:

LongeviTea—"for the far sighted"—contains: Siberian Ginseng, Sarsaparilla, Fo Ti, Hawthorne, Nettles, Ginko, Gotu Kola, Licorice, Alfalfa, Oatstraw, and Violet. There's no better time than now to start planning for your future. LongeviTea contains herbs traditionally used for long life and health.

ImmuniTea—"strengthens your vitality"—contains: Rosehips, Lemon Grass, Peppermint, Ginger, Elder Flowers, Echinacea Root, Slippery Elm Bark, Licorice, Astragalus, and Thyme. ImmuniTea has herbs traditionally used for tonifying the body's own natural defenses and helping to prevent or recover from colds and flus.

There are a dozen of these blends including LeviTea, Mental ClariTea, PuriTea, and so forth, each one a complex blend of common and unusual herbs long associated with the condition the tea aims to deal with. We tried several of them, have served them to our guests and, without fail, are always asked, "Where'd you get that great tea?" My only complaint is that the teas are not yet that easy to find in markets in our area.

The blends are the work of owner Brigitte Mars, one of a group of modern American herbalists determined to bring herbs back into their rightful places in America: on the kitchen and bathroom shelves of our homes.

Brigitte has worked for years at Alfalfa's, a large, almost fancy, natural whole foods store in Boulder. She still spends one day a week in their herb department, and also writes on herbs, teaches in her area and around the country about herbs, has a local radio program on natural medicine, and makes and sells audio tapes on herbs.

The idea for the tea company came to Brigitte Mars as she sat through an Alfalfa's business meeting a few years ago, a meeting at which she had expected to make a presentation that would allow her to be sent to a trade show for the company. She prepared for the meeting, she says, by drinking her own home-made special herb tea, took a small overdose of vitamins, amino acids, and herbs, wore rosemary oil and a yellow shirt (to keep her own brain stimulated), walked to work to pump up with oxygen, and then sat there ready for everything—and nothing happened.

"Lots of overhead charts, lots of boring numbers. I was sitting there with my own circuits all lit up and nothing else to think about and somehow rather easily thought about doing a tea called mentalclaritea. The meeting went on and on, and I thought of one called serenitea, and what I might try blending for that. By the end of the meeting I had put the tea company idea together and went home to talk to my husband about it."

Husband Tom was into department store construction at the time and often feeling ill from using too many chemicals in products at his work. He was definitely open to a new adventure. Brigitte worked with herbs every day at the store and noticed that her customers would ask her advice and then easily become baffled if she named too many herbs. Starting a little tea company, they decided, would be a great way to put some of their own ideas out there into the business world. They wanted to see if they could build a company that put real quality into its product, that could produce a decent living for its owners and employees, and that didn't cause very much harm at all to the environment. So far, they are succeeding far beyond their original dreams.

One of the main issues all herbal product makers must confront is the issue of the quality, of the herbs that are used in an edible, drinkable product. If you grow and dry your own herbs you have no doubt about the quality, but you also quickly realize how limited are your supplies of fresh, organically grown herbs, particularly in the varieties necessary to produce complicated formulas for products like blended teas.

UniTea turned to Trout Lake Farm in Washington state, the largest organic herb grower in the U.S., but they look constantly for other organic growers who can handle the orders the company needs. Small growers contact Siddall all the time wanting to grow one or two crops for the company, but they are usually not big enough, says Siddall, or they don't have the capacity to dry the herbs to the company's specification. Proper drying, he says, is every bit as important for tea makers as the herb growing itself.

"We are extremely picky," says Siddall, "because we have to be. We want a very reliable source, very consistent, and we want certified organics, tested in a laboratory. Everyone says they are growing organically, but we need to be more careful than that. First of all, the quality and strength of the herbs is far greater if they are grown organically. If you introduce agricultural chemicals into the product, the potency of the herbs can be changed completely. Secondly, if we are going to be dealing with a tough FDA we, too, need to be tough, just to protect ourselves and put out the product we claim."

UniTea does buy herbs from other companies, and does even buy some herbs from overseas. But they usually do their import purchasing through Trout Lake Farm whose owners have visited the overseas herb farms and feel they can vouch for the suppliers. They are working hard to have 100 percent certified, organically grown, U.S. supplied herbs as soon as possible.

UniTea would also like to see herbs even more graded and rated than they are. "Perhaps we can get like the Chinese, eventually," says Pfeiffer, and grade medicinal herbs by the climate and soil they are grown in, by the process and the time of their harvesting, and how they are processed. Good Chinese pharmacists, he says, can tell these things about herbs simply by looking at them, and herbs from there are priced accordingly.

Meanwhile, UniTea has developed nearly 800 store accounts, some who use only three tea varieties, some with the full 12 choices. They realize they could double or triple their business easily if they went to tea bags, as most Americans are still hooked on pre-packaged foods, but so far the company is looking at other ways to branch out rather than to get into heavy packaging.

Brigitte does most of the selling to stores by telephone. They have a list of all the health food stores around the country and she simply calls them up to see if they are interested in trying bulk medicinal teas. Those who are interested receive a package of samples in little plastic bags with the beautiful labels on each one, plus some company literature. The best seller by far is the tea called ImmuniTea.

Brigitte gives seminars at stores around the country, speaks at conventions, and also does week-long herb programs at retreat centers such as the Omega Center in New York. She is involved in the start-up of a local herb school, The Rocky Mountain Center for Botanical Studies, and they are also members of the Rocky Mountain Herbalist Coalition.

The company has strict rules with themselves: they never borrow money, won't let investors in yet, and say they want to grow the company the way they expect farmers to grow their herbs: organically—and with the roots deep and strong first. They won't allow themselves, or anyone else, to work more than 36 hours a week, and they remain as flexible as possible about time off. This work, they say, "shouldn't ruin our lives." They hope to hang on to these ideas as the company grows larger.

At the time of our visit they were considering the purchase of a hammer mill so that they could more easily deal with small growers by being able to process a few of the ingredients themselves. For now they use a counter top Vitamix® machine when they need to make some ingredients smaller.

The teas are mixed in the back room following Brigitte's little 3"x5" recipe cards. The ingredients are weighed and put in a 20-gallon bucket and mixed by hand. The stores get color coded, beautifully labeled half-gallon jars with the opening orders, along with the smaller crack and peel labels, plus the little plastic jars, for customers to take home. The teas wholesale for from $10 to $16 dollars per pound with a suggested retail price of nearly double that. Most retail customers buy only a few ounces at a time.

When asked for advice for those who would try tea blending on their own, Brigitte is encouraging and cautious. Learn each individual herb, she says, making teas with just that one until you learn the taste and the effect. Remember the importance of aroma. Be sure you understand the herb and its possible effects so that you don't, for example, mix a stimulant with a sedative. Try to be certain you start with the very best herbs possible; get real quality in growing, harvesting, and drying.

When you are blending teas, she adds, try them on yourself and then on your family and friends—listening carefully to their comments. It can easily take 10 tries or more to get even a simple blend that is both helpful and tasteful. Be sure to keep your teas stored in glass jars away from heat and light, so that they won't lose aroma or color. Don't boil the water when making teas, she advises.

"Bring water to a boil and remove it from the source of heat, then add 1 heaping teaspoon of herb per cup of water for steeping. Stir and cover. It is best not to use a tea ball. Allowing the herbs to circulate freely in the water maximizes the potency of the water infusion. Strain out the herbs after steeping."

Relax and enjoy.

Herbs, Etc., Santa Fe

NOW WE COME to an especially interesting herbal product, liquid herbal extracts, and the whole complicated controversy that is swirling around the country as I write this, over the issue of labeling, health claims, the Federal Drug Administration (FDA)—and who's in charge of your health care and your medication.

First of all, the product itself. If you are interested in all things herbal, you have very likely noticed, as I have in the last couple of years, that it is becoming common to sit down at a restaurant or coffee shop with friends and to have them whip out a little amber colored one-ounce bottle and put a few drops of an herbal extract, often echinacea drops, into their soft drink or water.

The taste is very herby, even a little on the weedy side, almost bitter, yet not at all unpleasant. Echinacea is a stimulant to the immune system, it helps the body produce more and stronger white blood cells, and an extract made from the root, leaves, and/or stems of certain echinacea plants has become the favorite way of ingesting this long-used herb, along with many other herbs and herbal formulas.

Liquid herbal extracts are easily taken, easily absorbed into the bloodstream and body. They are also relatively inexpensive (about seven or eight dollars a bottle) and now more and more people swear by them for both the prevention and containment of colds and flu, and in the treatment of many common health problems usually treated by over-the-counter remedies.

Our visit to an herbal extract manufacturer was to Herbs, Etc., of Santa Fe, New Mexico, a company that started in 1970 under the direction of a well known herbalist and teacher, Michael Moore, and has been owned and operated by Daniel Gagnon since 1982.

Gagnon is a French Canadian and third generation business-man who spent lots of his early life in hospitals and at doctor's offices, with severe conditions of allergy, asthma, and eczema. His own illness led him into the study of herbalism and caused him to open a natural food store in northern Ontario in the early '70s. There he introduced yogurt and brown rice to the local population, taught cooking classes, and continued his ever more serious study of herbs and naturopathic medicine.

Gagnon came to Santa Fe in 1979, discovered the herbal teaching of Michael Moore, and decided that he "wanted very much to learn from this man." He went repeatedly to the little company Moore owned to ask for work and finally, after many refusals, got a job packaging lavender in little one-ounce bags. But at least he was inside the door, learning from Moore and also learning that the small company was suffering from Moore's inattention. "Michael Moore is an amazing, incredible, and knowledgeable herbalist and teacher. He's just not a business-man." But Gagnon was, and is. He bought the company in 1982 and set about turning it into one of the largest extract companies in the country.

The process of making the extracts begins at the back door of this small manufacturing plant in Santa Fe with the (usually) air freight arrival of freshly grown herbs from locations all around the country. This point also begins what Gagnon considers his most important contribution to the business: the good manufac-turing processes that keep his company in the black, out of trouble with the FDA, and growing at 25 to 35 percent per year.

First comes a botanist's identification of the material, to see not only that the plant is what it is supposed to be, but also that it has strong medicinal properties and is not a weak cultivar. Sec-ondly, a sample is quickly dried, given a lot number, so as to be easily identified through the manufacturing process, and so that every batch is thus traceable. Then the sample is bagged for stor-age and held for three years.

The material itself is extracted in one of two ways: one is the maceration method where the green fresh herbs are first ground in a vertical cutter machine and put into a large container with water and alcohol. There they sit and soak for (usually) two weeks. The other method is called percolation, and involves grinding whole dried herbs in a hammer mill, packing those ground herbs into glass funnels, and slowly adding alcohol and water that then percolate (at room temperature) and drip through the herbs, drawing out the active properties of the plants.

Gagnon is especially proud of the speed of the first part of these methods—that they process the herbs immediately after receiving and grinding. The company literature tells the story:

"The herbs are slowly ground mechanically without heat, and within minutes are placed in the extraction process. This procedure and timing are extremely important because the biggest loss of potency of the active ingredients occurs after the herbs are ground....(and) the extraction process used by HERBS, ETC. is a cold process. Absolutely no heat is ever used since heat is very damaging to the potency of the active ingredients."

After careful filtering of the liquids, they are poured into the small one-ounce amber colored jars, droppers are added, the jars are labeled, set with a shrink sleeve sealer and then sent to the shipping department. Two samples of each batch are held back: one set aside for the FDA in case they should ask for it, the other sample for the company so that they have a sample of every batch made by either process.

The size of the large shipping department gives a clue as to how well the company is doing, and also reveals the company's commitment to the environment—the same commitment we found in one small company after another while making our rounds. Herbs, Etc. used to ship in nice little white boxes. No more. Gagnon returned to brown kraft boxes, because of the bleach needed to produce white paper. He bought a shredder and now uses shredded newspapers for all the packing. Every two weeks a local gardener picks up the batches of compressed herbs that have come through the percolation system and takes them home to compost.

The company actually sells different labels to two markets because the health professionals who use the products—acupuncturists, naturopaths, and yes, MDs—don't like the products they offer to their clients, says Gagnon, to be available under the same label at the corner health food shop. The company label for the professional market is called Naturae Medica.

Importantly, the company also has a little retail herb shop in downtown Santa Fe where Gagnon's very experienced employees keep a one-on-one relationship going with the increasing numbers of the public who are turning to herbal product use as another choice in their own health care.

"The truth is," says Gagnon, "that 37 million people in this country don't have any health insurance. They know it could cost maybe $75 to see the doctor and another $50 for medicine that may or may not work for them. If their friends are having good luck using herbal products, chances are they will give it a try, too. And, if it works for them, they become converts. After all," he continues, "people are really getting disillusioned with orthodox medicine. And they don't like just waiting to get sick and then having crisis medicine. They want to build themselves up a little bit by trying some preventive medicine."

Herbs, Etc.'s retail shop in downtown Santa Fe

The other thing going for the herb shop is that New Mexico itself has a long history of herbal practices. "This is New Mexico," says Gagnon, "Land of Enchantment, which means that there is a *curandero*, an herbal healer, for every few people. It is a part of the heritage of both the Indians and the Hispanics. They still use their own osha, their epazote, their *herba negrita* for their hair. It's a part of who they are. Herbs are completely normal here."

Gagnon also works closely with Santa Fe doctors. "If someone comes to us in the shop and doesn't know what they have, we send them to a doctor. Doctors are great label slappers. Go get a label, we say, and then come back and we can probably help you. That also helps us rule out cancer and other very serious diseases. Of course, we can offer supportive treatment for such cases, but personally I do not believe that an herbalist working in a shop should be treating such a person."

Besides the single herb extracts, Gagnon has developed a line of herbal extract formulas that are also becoming better and better sellers. These, too, come from working with customers in the shop. The Santa Fe Opera singers have been long time customers. They would come into the shop and say, "Listen to this croak of mine, and I've got to sing tonight. What can you give me to help?" For four years Gagnon worked with them developing an extract he calls Singer's Saving Grace which he now ships to singers and speakers all over the country.

He reads constantly about herb studies from all over the world; his office library is one of the best I've ever seen. He runs his company primarily on the Deming Principles, business methods first promoted by Edwards Deming who visited and helped turn around Japanese industries in the early '50s and '60s. Deming then came back to try and tell America about his revolutionary approach to the business practices he had been applying there.

Incremental steps towards improvement are at the basis of the Deming method. You examine every tiny step and procedure in the business itself and look to make improvements there. Nothing earth-shaking, but always towards a smoother, more efficient step in the process.

At Herbs, Etc., that has meant having a little notch put in the insert that goes in the shipping box so that the packer can pack the box more smoothly. It has meant switching box manufacturers to find one to make a box that would hold the bottles more snugly so the labels would never rub off. And on and on, one small step looked at each time, with the improvements almost constant and the problems always being examined. A kind of continual quality control that has finally caught on in many companies in America, and that Gagnon practices with great pride.

And he deals often with the FDA. Of course they visit, he says, they wouldn't be doing their jobs properly if they didn't.

One of the most encouraging things about the new breed of American herbalists, like Gagnon and others we have met and read about in our research for this book, is their strong determination to see that the subject of medicinal herbalism in this country is brought in from the counter-culture corner and made to stand in full view on its own scientific base. And they stress the importance of the herb industry setting higher standards for itself, investigating all reports of any herb induced illness or problem; the use of extreme caution in recommending any herbs (such as comfrey and, these days, chaparral) that have any history of reported problems—even minor ones. It is not enough simply to say that even aspirin is known to have caused illness and, occasionally, deaths; that doctors prescribe medicine every day for people that sometimes does far more harm than good. The herb industry, they believe, must become ever more responsible in its own practices.

But in the midst of trying to put this solid base under herbalism based on the present day sciences of botany, chemistry, and medicine, the whole industry has had to stop and take up arms against the FDA, and its attempts to shove the whole idea of herbs and plant-based medicines back into the dark corners of pseudo-science.

At the time of our visit to Santa Fe, Daniel Gagnon was one of many herbalists around the country involved in a serious campaign to prevent the FDA from placing severe limitations on the marketing of dietary supplements in this country. And for the FDA, vitamins, minerals, amino acids, fatty acids, plant and fish oils, and **most herbs** are placed in the category of dietary supplements and due to come under a very strict set of laws severely controlling the labeling of the products and limiting any health claims that can be made in their behalf.

In Europe, and especially in Germany, where a long herbal tradition has remained strong, drugstore shelves carry endless herbal preparations alongside more recent chemical preparations. The customer can choose whatever seems applicable, and insurance companies reimburse for herbal medicines and treatments, just as they do for allopathic, or ordinary medicine. But in the U.S. , where the everyday use of herbs fell along the wayside in the mid-twentieth century, it is becoming somewhat of a tough political battle to allow the reappearance of this custom.

In Europe, plant-based medicines are acceptable because of a long tradition of use and because of a long-standing agreement on the physiological effect of many herbs. This so-called "doctrine of reasonable certainty" means that plant-based medicines can be put on the shelves without the costly tests required in the U.S. There is a GRAS, or "generally agreed as safe" list in the U.S. that includes some herbs, primarily culinary herbs, that is approved by the FDA, but the list is quite limited and many now relatively popular herbs in products are not covered by that list.

Of course, the stakes are incredibly high. Once herbal products are forced to seek drug classification, and many feel that that seems to be what the FDA is aiming for, the testing required for each could cost something over $250,000,000 per product. This testing system is run for patentable products, products that can be marketed with exclusivity for some time. Furthermore, chemicals produced in manufacturing plants are the chemicals that these expensive drug tests are set up to monitor—not the more complex chemicals found in most herb plants.

Writing in a recent issue of *The Business of Herbs*, Steven Foster, a noted authority on medicinal plants worldwide, reminds us that the existing procedures for testing drugs would never even be applicable for herbs, because herbs "are complex multi-chemical substances (over 100 chemical components in the essential oil of rosemary, alone, for example). The application process is set up for *single isolated chemical compounds*."

The products of Herbs, Etc., are one tiny example of a growing phenomenon in this country, recently revealed in national polls, that found that over 30 per cent of all patients of the average American doctor also seek medical help from other, non-traditional sources, such as chiropractors, acupuncturists, massage therapists, and herbalists. Added to that, the enormous over-the-counter, or non-prescription drug business in America is being ever-so-slightly challenged of late by the rising popularity of dietary supplements and herbal medicine. This is especially true in the area of prevention, which has only recently even become a topic of discussion in mainstream medical circles. Nowadays, millions of Americans are trying, on their own, to prevent illness by the increased use of vitamins and herbs—based on information they are getting from many different sources.

At this moment, we are all hearing from many media sources about the subject of anti-oxidants and their cancer fighting abilities. At the same time, we are also learning, mostly on our own, that the best anti-oxidant producers in our diet are foods with high concentrations of beta carotene (vitamin A), and vitamins C and E. Many, many people are beginning to supplement their diets with daily doses of these vitamins. Should vitamin manufacturers be able to tell us in their marketing about this connection with anti-oxidants?

Apparently not, according to the FDA's new proposals, which the herb and other supplement industries are fighting. As of this writing, two bills are pending, one in each house of congress, that would soften this hard-line approach and would still offer consumers a choice in purchasing dietary supplements so long as the labeling and advertising is truthful and non-misleading and that there exists a reasonable scientific basis for product claims. But no matter how this argument turns out, American consumers long ago decided for more choices (not fewer) in their own health care. The FDA may be able to squash and squeeze some products from the market at this time but in their efforts they have aroused so many consumers that I doubt if their findings would hold for long.

Daniel Gagnon has been a part of this effort to fight the new FDA rules: he helped in the first of what have become nation-wide *black-outs* in health food and herb shops around the country. On a given day the stores in one region will refuse to sell all the products that would be affected by the new FDA regulations. The customers become outraged and write their congressmen, the shop owners become educated on just what such legislation can mean to them, and the congressmen and women hear from many thousands of constituents. With that kind of grass roots organization, I just don't think such a tightening of regulations can last for too long.

Meanwhile, Daniel Gagnon's business flourishes, along with almost every other herb business we visited, as the American consumer becomes ever more sophisticated about herbs. When I first started selling culinary herbs 10 or 12 years ago, I seemed always to be teaching people how to tell the difference between oregano and marjoram, or how to make basil pesto. But the times they are a changin'. Nowadays, a young acquaintance presents me with a bottle of echinacea drops she has produced from her own plant roots; another recommends arnica salve for my husband's sore knee, and says she spent her summer vacation at an herbal school in Wyoming. Still another calls to ask me where he can get *ma huang* (Chinese ephedra). There is such a ground swell across the land for these wondrous plants in every form that I don't think anyone or anything can stop it. At the very same time there is an equally strong push by more people every day, for a variety of reasons, to start their own small businesses. Now these two forces are coming together all across the country in a burgeoning of herbal businesses. In my humble opinion, we ain't seen nothin' yet. Hooray!

Herbal Product References

ASSOCIATIONS

American Herbal Products Association, PO Box 2410 Austin, TX 78768. 512-320-8555. FAX 512-320-8908.

The primary herbal product association. Membership starts at $250 per year for gross annual sales of $500,000 or less. It is a fast growing group and has been extremely active in the current controversy with the FDA on new labeling laws. Members can be those who sell, import, manufacture, or supply herbs or herbal products and information.

Nutritional Health Alliance, PO Box 267, Farmingdale, NY 11735. 516-249-7070.

An organization created within the herbal and health food products network to organize resistance to the FDA efforts to tightly regulate the sales of herbal, vitamin, and supplement products. $25 for yearly membership. New members may call 800-226-4NHA to join.

PUBLICATIONS

If there's not a sample copy price listed, that does not mean there's not one available. Most publications will send a sample copy (often for a fee, sometimes not) if you contact them by phone or by mail.

Natural Foods Merchandiser. Published monthly by New Hope Communications Inc., 1301 Spruce St., Boulder, CO 80302. 303-939-8440. FAX 303-939-8440. $44 per year.

A large-format, slick magazine aimed primarily at store product buyers and full of ads and information on green and natural food and health products. A fine way to track the movement of products and companies in this growing market. Articles on regulations, industry trends and company news. Also announces expos and trade shows. Sample copy $10.

The Crafts Report. Published monthly. $24 yearly from 700 Orange St., PO Box 1992, Wilmington, DE 19899. 302-656-2209. Toll Free 800-777-7098.

Strongly oriented to helping crafts people make more sales. National retail shows and fairs listed monthly, plus national and international wholesale shows that crafters may be interested in. They also offer suggestions on business forms, contracts, and law for crafts people.

Craft Supply Magazine. The industry journal for the professional crafter. Published four times per year. $40 per year from Box 420, Englishtown, NJ 07726-9982. 908-446-4900. FAX 908-446-5488.

January issue is an annual directory. Other three issues list wholesale and retail shows nationwide, plus lots of info for crafts people wanting to become more serious in taking their products into a larger market. Many and varied ads all aimed at crafters of all kinds.

Organic Food Business News. Published monthly. $84 yearly from Hotline Printing and Publishing, PO Box 208, Williston, ND 58802.

A newsletter format with monthly news on marketing organically grown produce and food products. Calendar section of food and agriculture shows, business news of farms and markets dealing in organic produce and food items, latest organic prices on herbs, etc., plus a close following of the issues surrounding the increasing demand for organically grown food in the American marketplace. Half-price subscriptions offered regularly to new subscribers. Sample copy, $2.

Marketing Crafts and Other Products to Tourists. A 12-page free guide from Publications Office, Cooperative Extension, Univ. of Neb., IANR Communications & Computing Services, Lincoln, NE 68583. (Growing For Market.)

U.S. Government Information. U.S. Dept of Agriculture, Agriculture Cooperative Service. ISS Rm 4209 So., PO Box 96576, Washington, DC 20090-6576.

You may write to them for a free packet of information especially for crafts people. It lists a number of programs in the federal government that may provide assistance to developing craft cooperatives and other small businesses. It lists various craft councils and associations, and several publications for craft producers.

World Convention Dates, Directory of Trade Shows, Meetings and Conventions. Published annually, and available through your library.

Lists trade shows worldwide by product category.

SUPPLIES

Action Bag Company, 501 N. Edgewood Ave., Wood Dale, IL 60191-1410. For ordering, 800-824-2247; in Illinois, call 708-766-2881. FAX 708-766-3548.

Resealable poly bags in many sizes, plain poly bags, cellophane bags, cloth drawstring bags, twist ties, paper bags, gift totes, colored tissue and gift wrap, shopping bags, plus custom printed bags, and more. Minimum order is $30. Accepts Visa and MC. Send for catalog.

The Bottle Solution, PO Box 3562, Boone, NC 28607. 704-262-5810. No minimums.

Carnaud Metalbox, 410-273-1890. FAX 410-273-1889. (Business of Herbs.)

Chiswick Trading Co., 33 Union Avenue, Sudbury, MA 01776-2267. Ordering information 800-225-8708. FAX 800-638-9899.

Poly bags, boxes, labels, mailing bags, and many other packaging products and shipping supplies. Catalog available.

Drug and Cosmetic Industry Catalog, PO Box 6150, Duluth, MN 55806. Price $25.

I have not seen this, but it is recommended by *The Business of Herbs*, as offering both packaging material and supplies, plus botanical ingredients.

Essential Oil Co., PO Box 206, Lake Oswego, OR 97034. 503-6976-5992. FAX 503-697-0615. Toll free ordering 800-729-5912.

Sells essential oils, flower waters, vegetable oils, natural flavor oils, perfume oils and miscellaneous incense, amber bottles, aroma diffusers, plus books on aromatherapy. $50 minimum or $5 service charge on smaller orders.

Excelsior Incense Works, 1413 Van Dyke, San Francisco, CA 94124. 415-822-9124.

Incense-making materials and books on making incense.

I F A R Wreath Rings & Supplies, 8424 Sunset Road N. E., Minneapolis, MN 55432. 612-784-0812. FAX 612-784-3497. Toll free ordering: 800-578-4327.

Sells wreath frames of all descriptions, crimpers, garland and bow making machines, ribbon, wreath decorations, more. Catalog available.

Lavender Lane, 6715B Donerail Dr., Sacramento Ca. 95842. 916-334-4400.

Glass bottles and jars, plastic bottles and jars in many shapes and sizes, plus fragrance oils, essential oils, plus soap making kits, and lots of odd bits, including tea bags, muslin drawstring bags, etc. Minimum shipping charge of $3.75. Catalog $2.

Nature's Finest, PO Box 10311, Burke, VA 22009. 703-978-3915.
Supplies for potpourri, perfume and cosmetic making. Catalog $2.50.

Olshen's Bottle Co., 923 S. Bayview, Seattle, WA 98134. 800-827-8819.

J. Rabinowitz & Sons, Inc., 1300 Metropolitan Ave., Brooklyn, NY 11237. 718-386-1000. Out of NY, call 800-354-2277.
Glass bottles and jars, plastic containers, packaging of all kinds. (Business of Herbs)

The Ribbon Factory Outlet, PO Box 405, Titusville, PA 13654. 814-827-6431. FAX 814-827-4191. (Business of Herbs)

The Soap Saloon, 7309 Sage Oak Ct., Citrus Heights, CA 95621. 916-723-6859.
They specialize in soap molds. Catalog $1.

Star West, 11253 Trade Center Dr., Rancho Cordova, CA 95742. 916-638-8100. To order, 800-800-HERB (4372).
Bulk supplies of dried herbs etc.

Steeltin Can Corp, 1101 Todds Lane, Baltimore, MD 21237. 410-686-6363. Color catalog.
Decorative tins.

Sunburst Bottle, 7001 Sunburst Way, Citrus Heights, CA 95621. Tel/FAX 916-722-4632.
They specialize in bottle ware, especially unusual items. No minimums. Minimum shipping charge of $3.75. Catalog is $2, refunded with first order.

Sunfeather Herbal Soap Co., HCR 84 Box 60A, Potsdam, NY 13676. 315-265-3648.
Soap making supplies and books.

Trout Lake Farm, 149 Little Mountain Road, Trout Lake, WA 98650. 509-395-2025.
The largest producer of certified organic herbs. Wholesale only to business. Minimums.

Whole Herb Co. PO Box 1203, Sonoma, CA 95476. 707-935-1077. FAX 707-935-3447.

Hundreds of different bulk botanical products plus essential oils, potpourri ingredients and blends.

See the **Herb Farm Reference** section for more on supplies.

RECOMMENDED VIDEOS

Herbal Preparations and Natural Therapies: Creating and Using a Home Herbal Medicine Chest, by Debra Nuzzi, M. H. Morningstar Publications, 177 Brook Circle, Boulder, CO 80302.

CONSULTANTS

Dr. James A. Duke, Economic Botanist, c/o 8210 Murphy Road, Fulton, MD 20759. 301-498-1175.

Willing to consult on formulating herbal products.

Jim Long, of Long Creek Herb Farm, Rt 4, Box 730, Oak Grove, AR 72660. 417-779-5450.

Willing to consult on Herb Farms, herb events, and herbal products.

INFORMATION

Federal Drug Administration, and other governmental authorities on products. **FDA Phone Numbers** for a few offices around the country: Seattle area, 206-483-4970; Philadelphia, 215-597-0537; Chicago, 312-353-9406; Dallas, 214-655-8100; New York, 718-965-5528; San Francisco, 415-556-2263. (Business of Herbs)

First of all, if you are making up a non-medical product that you only intend to sell locally, through your farmers' markets or even to a local store, you should not need to contact the FDA. But you should contact your local or county health department to learn the rules concerning your product. If your product needs an OK from your state agriculture department, or any other state regulatory agency, your county health agent will let you know that and tell you how to contact the state agency. If you intend to sell your product (any food, drug, cosmetic, or medical device) across the country, or even in one other state, you should check in, by phone, with a compliance officer of the FDA. They will give you details about compliance based on the information you give them about your product. Often they will have you contact a government printing office for specific details on compliance for your particular product. One primary rule to be aware of is that no specific, unproven health claim can be made on any product. That means any claim whatsoever that the product has therapeutic value.

As far as the latest **nutritional labeling law** is concerned, food product businesses doing less than $50,000 annually need not comply with these new rules, and there are other exemptions possible in certain instances. But the old rules, about exactly how the ingredients must be listed on your label, still apply. Your FDA compliance officer, your local or county health officer, or your state agricultural officer can give you more details on this. Be patient in this area. Be persistent, be accurate. If you are developing a product, take the time and learn the details. That's always where the devil hides out.

The 1993 Nutrition Labeling Regulations are available *free* from the attorney offices of **Collier, Shannon, Rill and Scott**, 3050 K Street, NW, Suite 400, Washington DC. 20007. 202-342-8400. When I wrote to them, they were working on a new edition with the most recent amendments added. That copy should be finished now.

Herb Dryer Plans. Complete plans for building a dryer are available from **Growing Edge Magazine**, PO Box 1027, Corvallis, OR 97339.

Ask for the Spring '93 issue (Vol. 4, #2) for $6.50. Or consider a subscription to this fairly high tech, but very interesting magazine about the latest ideas in small to medium home and commercial growing operations; from growing Shiitake mushrooms indoors, to hydroponic growth for herbs and flowers. I find it fascinating. Quarterly. $17.95.

HERBAL PRODUCT BUSINESSES

Dona Flora Herbs & Flowers. Beth Hailey, PO Box 77, La Conner, WA 98257

Maine Balsam Fir Products. Wendy & Jack Newmeyer, PO Box 9, West Paris, ME 04289

UniTea Herbs. Brigitte Mars & Tom Pfeiffer, PO Box 8005 #318, Boulder, CO 80306

Herbs, Etc. Daniel Gagnon, 1340 Rufina Circle, Santa Fe, NM 87501

RECOMMENDED BOOKS

Almost all of these should be available through your library. Be sure to also consider the books in the other reference sections.

The Complete Book of Herbs, by Lesley Bremnes. Viking Penguin Books, 1988.

An English herb enthusiast giving great recommendations on many things herbal. Good photographs of herbs at all stages—excellent for identification. An unusual section for decorative herbal arts including directions for making herbal inks and papers, herbal garlands and baskets, herbal dyes, plus a nice section on herbal beauty and bath products. An informative section on essential oils and their uses, a short but informative section on herbal preparations and herbal medicine. A good inspirational book for thinking about herbal products.

The Book of Potpourri, by Penny Black. Simon and Schuster, New York, 1989.

Recommended in the reference section on Herb Farms, this is also a fine book to use for ideas on getting started with herbal products. Very detailed examples in making scented sachets and sweetbags, herbal pillows, pomanders, tussie mussies and other scented flower arrangements, plus an informative section on drying herbs and flowers for use in products.

Selling What You Make: Profit From Your Handcrafts, by James Seitz. Tab Books, Blue Ridge Summit, PA, 1993.

The accent here is on selling, plus lots of general small business advice that recognizes the current trend towards home businesses in America. For the small operator, and anyone looking for a fairly large production business from their handcrafts, the book is thorough with very up-to-date consumer-oriented selling tips.

You Can Make Money From Your Arts and Crafts, by Steve and Cindy Long. Mark Publishing, Scotts Valley, CA, 1988.

This book has a nice approach to making, packaging and selling your own homemade products. If you are just considering getting into herbal products, I would recommend you read this first. The chapters on pricing and packaging are especially helpful, and much of the focus of the book is on craft shows and sales with some additional chapters on mail order selling and getting into wholesaling. A down to earth approach with both a ring of authenticity and a fine touch of humor.

Gifts From The Herb Garden, by Emelie Tolley and Chris Mead. Clarkson Potter, New York, 1991.

When your interest and creativity flag, turn to the Tolley-Mead herb books for a lift up and out of the ordinary. They teach you to make everything from eau de cologne and hand lotions to dried pepper wreaths and tussie mussies. And the photographs they use are even more helpful than the recipes they give. Superb.

Country Wines: Making and Using Wines From Herbs, Fruits, Flowers & More, Garden Way Publishing, Pownal, Vermont, 1992.

A fascinating little book for beginning wine makers, with a chapter on herbal wine making (from agrimony to woodruff), and an especially interesting chapter on making vinegars from wine musts, with recipes for all.

Flower Drying With A Microwave, by Titia Jooster. Sterling Publishing, New York, 1989.

A very detailed manual for drying flowers and foliage rather quickly in silica gel in a microwave. A small book, originally written in Dutch, it has some colored pictures plus line drawings. Lots of lists.

The Art of Soap Making, by Merilyn Mohr. Camden House Publishing, Ontario, 1988.

A brief history of soap making, then a chapter on natural lathering plants (those containing saponins), followed by fairly detailed steps for making soap. Lots of ingredient explanations and sources, plus recipes for basic test soaps in small amounts. Also gives very specialized soap recipes.

The Herbal Tea Garden, by Marietta Marshall Marcin. Storey Communications, Vermont, 1993.

All about tea and herbal tea plants, how to grow and use them, plus lots of history and information on medicinal uses of teas.

From Kitchen To Market, Selling Your Gourmet Food Specialty, by Stephen F. Hall. Upstart Publishing, Dover, NH, 1992.

You figure out how to make that great tasting herbal jelly no one else has been able to do, you first give it as gifts and then sell it successfully in your area at craft shows and the local farmers' market. Then you start to wonder about the possibility of putting it on the shelves of your gourmet shop, even your supermarket shelf. At that point, read this book. Hall takes you directly into the specialty food business of America and tries to help you decide if you belong there with your product. He covers pricing in some real detail, modern food labeling details, the food distribution system and how to fit into it, the food trade show scene, plus other food manufacturing subjects such as co-packers—those firms that will make up your food product to your specific recipes, while you pay attention to the important areas of sales and distribution. This book is a real eye opener into the deal making and tough competition in the American food industry today.

The Great American Idea Book, by Bob Coleman & Deborah Neville. W. W. Norton & Co., 1993.

This is for people who worry about protecting what they produce with patents, copyrights, registered trademarks, and so forth. Written by a patent attorney and a writer, this fits into the current emphasis on worldwide intellectual property rights. Also contains interesting sections on music, film and book writing, including ways to get your product in front of a wider audience. Very *Inc. Magazine* oriented.

WILD-CRAFTING

American wildcrafting is as old as

America: early settlers did trapping

in the winter, collected food and other

usable or salable material from the

wilderness the rest of the year.

Wildcrafting

As I write this, the chanterelle mushroom season is just beginning here in the Pacific Northwest, and the radio is full of news bits about the mushroom pickers, the prices they will get this year, and where the buyers are stationed near the forests.

It's a grand thought, isn't it, to consider earning your keep by merely collecting what is freely growing in the forest? But then the announcer goes on to interview some of the pickers who now choose to go armed into the forest to defend their area of national forest land, and that brings up one of the other, down sides of this outdoor collecting, or wildcrafting, as it is called among herbalists.

American wildcrafting is as old as America: early settlers did trapping in the winter, collected food and other useable or salable material from the wilderness the rest of the year. In my own recent days as a small commercial flower grower, I often collected bouquet additions from the wild and wrote about that, with some caution, in a book on flower growing and selling (see page 69). Long ago I heard about seed houses buying from those who would collect wildflower seeds, and talked my husband into going out with me on a few weekends to collect daisy seeds from fields near our home along the Pacific coast. It was fun for a few hours—which is about how long it took to realize just how very slowly those tiny seed pods would build up in our shoulder seed bags, and that this was probably not going to be our future.

But I have to admit I was momentarily smitten with the idea of working outdoors, taking a natural resource that seemed so abundant and was such easy picking, and one that someone, somewhere would pay us for.

That's what the mushroom pickers are all about, too, but in these days of high unemployment, along with high prices paid for exotic mushrooms, the stage has been set for just what has developed: turf wars in the national forests that have already resulted in a couple of shootings as more and more people go "out there" looking for edible mushrooms and spendable dollars.

All through our trips across the country to visit herb businesses, the subject of wildcrafting was often brought up, by those who do collect part or all of their herbs from the wild, by those who shun such products in their own work, and by those who work towards establishing an ethical approach to wildcrafting by the herb industry—an approach they feel will allow a continued and sustainable yield to be taken from the wild.

It's time to give expression to all of those opinions now in the telling about the work of three wildcrafters we visited. You will no doubt start to form your own opinion on wildcrafting based on these stories.

Native Scents, Inc., Taos

FIRST OF ALL, I must say right off that the wholesale brochure of this little company in New Mexico is splendid: a pocket-fold envelope of colorful Native American designs on heavy stock paper that opens up to a half dozen individual sheets of product pictures and price lists. Even if you weren't interested in the products themselves, the brochure would certainly tempt you.

It has tempted the buyers from the shop at the Smithsonian Institution in Washington, DC, and hundreds and hundreds of other shops around the country that now feature Native Scents' incense logs and wands, sweetgrass braids, wrapped smudge bundles, dream pillows, sachets and other Native American products. The company was just reaching their first million dollar sales year at the time of our visit.

Al Savinelli, a youngish half-Chippewa from Minnesota, owns (most of) and runs Native Scents, whose products are primarily based on field-collected material. The collecting is done by both Al and "*a co-op network of Native American wildcrafters who collect plants in a conscious way, respecting the ecological habitats and local traditions.*" Most of the company's actual employees in Taos are also Native Americans, some from the nearby Taos Pueblo.

Al taught himself to make incense years ago. His first efforts "looked just like duck droppings," as he worked towards making an inexpensive product that would sell more easily and in greater quantity than the one-of-a-kind animal skin and fibre art pieces he had been making and selling at craft and art shows.

Al has been making and selling incense and sage bundles for almost 20 years. Now, suddenly, the whole Native American thing has taken off, sweeping him and his little company right into success.

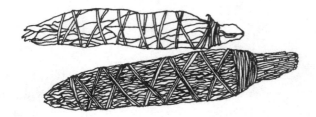

Smudge bundles

"What was esoteric even ten years ago," he says, "is now completely mainstream. And that's happening all over the country, all over the world. Twenty years ago no one knew anything but salt, pepper, and ketchup. Now the biggest selling flavorings are salsa and chili peppers." He laughs with the joy and amazement of someone who looks around to see that at least a part of the world has caught up with his own taste and values.

The botanical products Native Scents collects from the wild include sage and juniper, osha root, mugwort, red willow bark, incense cedar leaf, copal (which is brought in from Guatemala) yerba santa, piñon pine, and sweetgrass (*Hierochloe odorata*).

For 20 years Al has been picking white sage in California; a few hundred pounds those first few years, now up to 8,000 pounds a trip, for which he needs a semi-trailer to carry and deliver it back to New Mexico. Besides collecting what his own company needs, he has also always sold to other herb companies around the country. These days wild white sage brings about $4 per pound, wholesale.

That sounds like such a big haul. Surely there are problems created in taking so much of a single plant. What if everyone went out and did that? Al laughs at the idea. "There's a very limited market for such a plant. And, much more importantly, a nearly unlimited supply of it on undeveloped land." He considers the loss of habitat for both plants and animals to be a far more important question than overpicking. That's the loss we need to pay attention to, he says, along with the question of biological diversity.

"I picked this year on eight acres near Riverside, California, that is scheduled to become a golf course. The trimmed plants recover their growth, in fact sage grows all the better for my picking, but once the housing or other development goes in, the land is lost forever to the natural possibilities."

Al agrees that there is a real problem in wildcrafting—created by opportunists who hear of the popularity of one herb or another, and then swarm all over an area, taking all they can, even picking up the last possible root, thus making certain that no crop can grow there again.

This has been especially true recently with plants like echinacea and goldenseal, both of which could long be found in wild tracts around the country. Jim Long, of Long Creek Herb Farm in Missouri, tells of watching young teenagers in pickup trucks in the Ozarks ripping up echinacea plants, throwing them into the back of the truck and roaring off to find someone to buy them—simply because they've heard the plants are valuable. All through North American history, trappers have been the wildcrafters of plants, taking both animals and plants in season, and living off the land in a relatively benign way. Most of the population never heard anything at all about wildcrafting, or the value of wild plants.

Nowadays, exotic stories get circulating about the use and value of certain plants and the plants themselves can become endangered rather quickly. Readers have probably all read and heard tales in recent years of ginseng root, and the exorbitant prices those roots bring—along with the danger to pickers (usually from other pickers) seeking that wild root. Jim Long tells of the recent appearance of a "news" article in his area claiming that goldenseal would mask drug use, so now truck stops along the main highways in his part of the country are carrying boards of little goldenseal capsules near the cash registers. According to several heath food store owners in Jim's area, other rumors about the use of goldenseal to enhance illegal drugs have also driven up prices. Wherever goldenseal is growing in the wild, pickers will be after it.

Long is one of many herbalists who are feeling conflicted by the wildcrafting issue. He collects morels and Ozarks dittany (*Cunila origanoides*) from his own land, but at our visit was beginning to feel that perhaps there must be more protective laws put in place for some of these species. As more and more Americans move outdoors for their recreation, they are taking a bigger interest in nature than ever before. Every summer, Jim says, when the butterfly weed is in bloom along the Missouri highways, the roadsides are filled with masses of tourists trying to pull up the plants even though the roots go down two or three feet, and the plants cannot be transplanted once the root is torn apart. Since our visit with Jim, new laws protecting roadside wild flowers and herbs now carry stiff fines for digging plants illegally in Missouri.

But more laws and rules are not wanted by many herbalists and some see that the bigger need is for serious herbalists to set higher standards among themselves and to support only ethical wildcrafters. Just such a group has already formed in Boulder, Colorado, called the Rocky Mountain Herbalist Coalition, "a regional group of herbalists, herb growers, wildcrafters, teachers, researchers, and manufacturers." They produce a direct-marketing registry of ethical wildcrafters and organic growers of medicinal herbs, to encourage a network of responsible herb-buying practices. They also offer ethical guidelines for wildcrafters, a list of botanists for specimen identification, and other useful information for anyone interested in the subjects of wildcrafting and medicinal herbs. Their address is listed in the reference chapter following this section on wildcrafting.

Daniel Gagnon, at Herbs, Etc. in Santa Fe, says that his company is going away from wildcrafted herbs because there can never be enough control in the wild to know that you are getting ethically harvested plants **and** organically grown plants. He believes the future is in learning to grow even the difficult-to-grow plants like ginseng and goldenseal, and in growing certified organic herbs.

"Organic farmers," he says, "know that they have to take care of their land and plan for the future. Too many wildcrafters haven't been educated that well. The farmer will protect his interest and take care of his land—the wildcrafter will simply move on to another place to pick."

Gagnon has purchased his first crop of certified organic osha root, and hopes by next year (he knocks wood in the telling) to have a crop of certified organic goldenseal.

"That's the future," he says, "because an ethical wildcrafter can go into a field of echinacea and only pick half. Another comes behind him and only picks half. Now we're down to a quarter and it will soon be down to an eighth and we all know where that's headed."

Al Savinelli agrees that there are those few plants that are seriously over-picked but claims that there are substitutes for most of them: Oregon grape (Mahonia nervosa) for instance, "is a perfectly viable chemical substitute for goldenseal, and that's a plant that could never be overpicked."

And always Savinelli returns to the protection of the land and the eco-system as the real way to protect specific plants. "Eighty five per cent of the world's population gets plant therapy," he says, "and now all that is being cut down, burned up, and built upon before we even find out what's out there."

He listens to the arguments about wildcrafting with a sad shrug, wishing the questions would go much deeper into the real problems he feels are threatening the great green pharmacies in the rainforests worldwide.

Meanwhile, back in New Mexico, Native Scents has some new products these days, ceremonial herbal teas, that take up Al's time and interest. He blends the teas and passes out cupfuls to the Native American workers in the big garage-like workshop that stands two blocks off the main highway through Taos. They take little bags of the teas home to taste-test with their families. The packaging costs for teas are so high that Al is learning to market the teas first in "little tie-up bags in Mom and Pop stores to see if the blends will sell." Only then, when the employees are happy with the taste and the little tie bags sell well, does he commit to the more expensive boxes for his main product line.

Al sees this business as virtually recession proof because the products are inexpensive to the consumer and bring real pleasure to people in their homes. "These products really do change the home environment. They are actually a part of the air freshener business—and that business is gigantic."

He travels every year to Central or South America and brings home tree resins, copal, and a few other products from those areas. He is intensely interested in native cultural issues all around the world, and is genuinely proud of his success in bringing Native American jobs to the Taos area, and in presenting Native American products in such a respectful and artistic fashion.

Brian Horne, Ladrona Island, Washington

"IT'S POISON OAK and poison ivy that will save the herbs," says Brian Horne, herbalist and wildcrafter extraordinaire.

"Most people don't take anything from the wild except photographs and then they leave their garbage behind. They're not interested in herbs. They're just afraid of poison ivy and poison oak. That's what saves the herbs from Sonoma County on northward. People stay out of the woods in droves because of those two plants. This worry over wildcrafters is a false concern. I see it as an exercise in a little bit of power and authority masquerading as worry and concern for the plants. It's utter piffle."

Meet the madcap, quick-witted, erudite herbalist of Ladrona Island. Ladrona is an isolated, non-ferry-served island off the coast of Washington near the Canadian border, where contact is primarily by mail boat IF you know where and when to pick that up and IF someone on Ladrona meets you at the dock to show you the way around the island. They don't welcome visits from tourists, so I've changed the island name; Brian doesn't welcome his work and life being interrupted, so I've changed his name, too.

"Most of my herbs come from this island which has no pesticide spraying, no polluting industry, no road or ferry access, no stores, no utilities, and no safe harbor. It is sparsely inhabited and over two miles of treacherous water from the nearest inhabited island. Many of my herbs come from never tilled land, especially steep seaside meadows, and from forests far away from human habitation and machines. My organically cultivated herbs are fertilized with seaweed, goat manure, maple leaves, and sea shells."

So reads Brian's single-spaced, single-page brochure, invoice, inventory sheet, and **only** paper message to the world of medicinal herb buyers. It is also full of small glimpses of the life and business style he has chosen to live on the high hilltop of this island of the San Juan Archipelago, in the sheltered waters of Northern Puget Sound:

"PREPAYMENT CAN CAUSE CONSIDERABLE DELAY."

"ISLAND HERBS is usually closed 20 December to 20 February each winter."

"In harvest season replies to postal inquiries other than simple orders can take up to 3 months."

"The dried herbs are dried by wood heat away from direct sunlight in rooms free of household and farm chemicals. My buildings and land have never received commercial pesticides."

"I go off island to ship UPS and use the phone at least once every two weeks, usually Monday."

"I collect monkey wrenches and believe in magick."

Enough to let you know, I think, that here is a wildcrafter worthy of herbal lore and literature. To visit with Brian Horne is to make a brief stop at a far different part of the world of herbs than most of us know. His one-person business provides some 40 wild products to herbal medicine makers around the country. His knowledge of and enthusiasm for the natural plant coverings of the earth is both astounding and entertaining.

With college degrees in chemistry and botany, plus post-doctoral training in cell biology, plus a decade of university teaching in botany and related subjects, Brian stands atop his little hillside on Ladrona in a stance of amused confidence—but always after having carried his daily gatherings (sometimes by the ton) up the steep hillsides to his hand-built cabin. He lives his own version of the Life of Riley that few of us would choose, but that most of us can't help but envy.

And his own lifestyle very much informs his vision of what wildcrafting is really all about.

Plants like echinacea and goldenseal, he believes, are sold only for effect. He avoids them like the plague. "They are tooooo powerful. Our problem isn't over-harvesting. It's a nutty culture."

He also avoids ginseng. "These are the herb world's magic bullets. Save them for emergencies. Putting these to everyday use is like asking God to do the dishes."

Some of our visit is spent harvesting the wild blossoms of St. John's Wort (*Hypericum perforatum*) because every visitor with a pair of hands can easily pick while they are learning about herbs. Brian has six to 12 apprentices come each year for a stay of learning and helping. Ruth picks with us today; she lives in a 36-foot school bus that Brian keeps on his 25 acres. The unopened floral buds we are picking give out a gorgeous burgundy liquid often used to make tinctures and salves. In a very lush stand, says Brian, he can pick eight or nine pounds per hour. But at our casual picking while talking rate, we are picking at a rate of about ½ lb. per hour each. Brian sells these blossoms for $20 per pound.

This plant has been outlawed in the Province of Ontario, he tells us, because it tends to take over the land and there are allegations that it causes photosensitivity in grazing animals. "I don't think so," says Brian, "but there **are** tiny little hairs on the plants that can irritate the eyes if you happen to wipe your brow while picking."

His harvesting is done all over the island, depending, he says with a smile, "on the current political situation." Ladrona Island is one of those few remaining places in this country where people choose to stay in isolation from the rest of society. There are perhaps eighty year-round residents, all of whom are probably somewhat extraordinary. It is definitely not a place a person would go to live if you didn't have a very strong sense of what you were all about, and what you could do to earn your living in such a non-commercial setting. Brian also does some picking on the other San Juan Islands.

Brian Horne is a compulsive, natural teacher. He recalls that as a youngster he was a nature lore teacher at summer camp, "and I'm still at camp!" His enthusiasm for the soil, the micro-climate, the amazing power of all these *weeds* around us simply pours out of him as he tells more than anyone can possibly take in. We pass a plant or two of Indian pipe (*Monotropa uniflora*) and he tells of its history, of its uses, the unusual way it attracts the roots of different trees to grow through it, the fact that it starts to bloom forth on St. John's Day and reaches its peak, and the beginning of its decline, always on Bastille Day, a few weeks after the solstice. He tells of a few well known herbalists around the country to whom he ships Indian pipe, and we both acknowledge that he is a part of a small group around the country now writing the new American herbalism based on modern science.

"After all, we're not living in *Gerard's Herbal* days," he says. "We have a very different reality. We are post DDT, post atomic bomb, post modern, if you will. "

The first few years of wildcrafting, he says, were very, very difficult, because he tried to keep his prices in line with other big suppliers. "'Red clover blossoms,' they'd say, 'why, we never pay more than 80 cents a pound for them.' Jeez, what a drag. I'd just spent two hours picking them, plus watching the kids—why, that's like 40 cents an hour."

Then he met Herbal Ed, Ed Smith of the Herb Pharm in Oregon, one of the most reputable herb dealers in the northwest. He thought Brian's products were excellent and encouraged him to raise his prices high and often. He could only use a little bit himself, but he sent other medicine makers to Brian for pollution free herbs and, in the 1980s, all those little businesses took off, and so then did Brian's business begin to grow. These days he charges $36 a pound for red clover blossoms and will be going up in price again soon, "although I never go up more than 10 percent a year. And I'll always give Herbal Ed first call on anything I have now."

Brian credits his years as a botanist preparing plant material for electron-microscopy with helping him prepare his plant materials for market. "I learned some tricks in those days that help me now. I was a small time authority on tissue preservation," and he now uses some of these tricks in his post-harvest handling of the herbs.

Brian considers his one-of-a-kind operation to be a business success in a small consistent way. He has resisted adding employees or "tying his children to the picking machine." He intends to stay a one-person operation because he just doesn't want the burdens that come with a larger business. "I have been relatively affluent in other times of my life and learned that bigger and better toys just don't do it for me. I had everything I wanted, and guess what?—it wasn't enough. Now the way I live is fun and cheap and low impact. "

We're near the top of his mountain now and his cabin looks out over miles of forest tops towards the sea, without a house or a road in sight. No plumbing, no electricity, no television, no stores; the impact of the place on the psyche is immediate and dizzy making. The spirit of Fletcher Christian seems near. I feel absolutely certain I could never live like this for very long, and feel just as strongly that I would love to try it. It's an Eden, all

Ladrona Island,
Washington

right, and tended by a man who has the sense to know it, and the brains to keep it together—barely.

The front part of the house itself is the herb dryer, kept at 105° with a constant fire in the wood stove. A tiny room at the back is the shipping room, piled with half-filled orders which Brian shuffles through. He packs the herbs in gallon zip-lock plastic bags, and accepts nothing smaller than a half-pound order.

He joined the International Herb Growers and Marketers Association "once, but I was buried in junk mail before I knew what hit me. I just couldn't handle that." So he un-joined and now even refuses up to thirty or forty per cent of his orders. "I certainly won't fill any orders from someone in a place like Los Angeles," he says. "Let them leave L.A. and then contact me. Anyone living there and trying to deal in pollution-free herbs is a fool. At least."

He can dry and handle up to a ton and a half every 8 to 10 days in the drying/shipping system he has, but he also earns a good percent of his income with seminars he teaches on Ladrona and at other places across the country. At our visit he was look-ing forward to a trip to Maine to speak at a conference there. And then one to Oregon to play a small part in the re-creation of the historical trip over the Oregon Trail.

He also earns a small part of his income from individuals who come and stay and study for a short time, although he admits that about half the people who come are gone in a week because they "can't stand the intensity and the lifestyle. I'm an over-doer, and besides, most people hate out-houses."

He has the most fun with the naturopathic students, who come to the island for weekend seminars after their three years of intensive, medical school education. They want to know about the plants that produce the medicines they will be using and "we get out there for 12 to 18 hours a day, do some harvesting, some intense work, camp outside—I love it. They love it."

Like other wildcrafters we have met, Brian remembers being a compulsive collector and harvester all his life. He grew up in

Des Moines, Iowa, and well remembers, as a child, when the pond at the cemetery was drained and he filled his red wagon with all the goldfish from there. His house now is surrounded by thousands of Indian stone tools he has collected as he walks the island every day.

Brian believes that too many herbalists promote endangered, rare herbs because they are the herbs that "have the greatest effect, not necessarily effectiveness—in terms of healing." He believes a wild plant is, by nature, much stronger than a domesticated or farmed plant "because it makes a willful decision to grow somewhere and is not just imposed into a place."

The most effective healing plants, he believes, are the ones that are generally thought of as weeds. Dandelions, yellow dock, St. John's Wort, chickweed, yarrow. "These are not only in abundance," he says, "but they are gaining ground. These are the true companion plants of the world." He also thinks people should be growing their own medicine in their yards, not always buying pills made in ways that destroy the environment. "And, if we all grew our own medicines, we sure wouldn't be using pesticides in our yards."

Yes, he admits, there are a few plants endangered by wildcrafting. "It's like collecting geniuses because you want to eat their brains. Eventually you'll run out of geniuses because, although they may be frequent, they are not abundant." But he doesn't spend a lot of time worrying about running out of this plant or that. People will use them all up if they are worth a lot of money and then we'll have to go on to something else. "After all," he muses, "Oregon grape has most of the properties of goldenseal, and we'll probably **never** run out of that plant. Or get rich selling it."

Brian realizes that people in the Rocky Mountains are trying to set up rules for wildcrafting because all around them they see "the crazies" coming in and sweeping over the land, taking whatever they can for quick dollars. Those are not wildcrafters. But he is one wildcrafter on five square miles who thinks that one real wildcrafter for every five square miles would hardly ever be noticed. "Now, five goats in one square mile," he grins, "that's different. That brings desertification—even out here." As far as Brian Horne is concerned, there are actually about eight true wildcrafters in the U.S. All the rest of this chit-chat is just that. And nonsense.

For anyone wanting to be a real wildcrafter, Brian advises that it will probably take up to five years to figure out what you are doing and to find some markets that are consistent and good to deal with. The markets were almost closed in the '70s, he says, and controlled by only a few large companies. "Their stuff sat around in bales for years.But these days there are more and more naturopaths in practice and many of them are wanting to make their own medicines. And wanting to use good stuff." He is also adamant that no one should be allowed to be a wildcrafter without a technical degree in biological sciences. "Then," he says, "if you do something biologically disruptive, you will have done it willfully, not just through ignorance."

As far as the controversy over wildcrafting is concerned, Brian believes that we are, as usual, paying attention to the wrong players. The real resource extractors in this country, he reminds us, are hardly the guys clipping St. John's Wort blossoms on some hillside. "Listen, when I go around in the spring and snip willow sprouts out of my neighbors' fields, they are damn glad to see me. I'm mowing their lawn. Those sprouts screw up their snapper cutters. If you've ever tried to snap cut an inch thick willow sprout, you would know just what I mean."

Yes, islanders do come to him for herbal self care. He never charges for it, and his two sons, ages 13 and 15, have never been to a doctor for a disease. The reason we all get into medical crises, Brian believes, is because we have asked doctors to be our "health parents," giving doctors both too great a burden that they really can't bear, and a very false sense of themselves. Knowledgeable self care, he believes, should be the basis for an American health care system. And from Ladrona Island, that makes perfect sense to me, too.

Marlin Huffman, Florida

LET'S GIVE SOME of the final words on wildcrafting to one who's been doing it a long, long time, and is one of the biggest and most successful in the country. Meet Marlin Huffman, of Plantation Botanicals, who began wildcrafting over 35 years ago, who brought up his children gathering plant materials along the roadsides and in vacant fields, and who, every few years, "would have to go to work as a professional farmer to get the family out of debt.

"In fact, we really lived in poverty for 25 years while I learned the art of wildcrafting," Marlin remembers, as we sit in his offices in tiny Felda, Florida, surrounded by greenhouses, trial plantings, dryers, and warehouses, with semi-trailers loading and unloading in the driveways

"But we accumulated some expertise in those 25 years, so that now we supply more than 50 percent of the world's needs for saw palmetto berries (*Serenoa repens*), and over 50 percent of the world's needs for passionflower (*Passiflora incarnata*). To be truthful, it took us nearly 30 years to get that far—so that the pharmaceutical companies around the world would even answer our phone calls, or let us in the door."

A large, friendly, self-educated man, sitting in a mobile home office in southwest Florida and wired into the floral and pharmaceutical markets of Europe, Latin America, and Asia, Marlin Huffman remembers back when he struggled to become a successful wildcrafter, and thinks about any advice he has to give to new would-be wildcrafters.

"Wildcrafting is a very, very tough business," he begins, "because you are totally at the mercy of your buyer. Let me give you one little example. You know the hibiscus plant, the one whose blossoms are used for herbal teas? A few years ago some European buyers came into Guatemala with some hibiscus seeds. They gave an acre of seeds and some fertilizer to several farmers there. At the end of the season, when they came back to buy, the farmers made about $800 each. That's about two years' worth of wages there. Then, the next year, the Europeans came back and offered seeds to anyone who wanted to grow hibiscus. Everyone who had heard any part of the $800 story wanted to grow the plants. You know the end of that story. The Europeans then came back and bought all they wanted for ten cents on the dollar. They caused overproduction and then they had total control.

Passionflower

"So the best advice I could probably give is to tell people to find something pretty close to the end user, and to find a way to sell it in a niche market. You have to think a lot about it, and it also takes a special kind of person to know what will work. People come to me all the time and say, what shall I do, what shall I go after? I don't think that the person who has to ask what to find is the one to succeed. Instead it is the person who is out there in the field, learning all the time, and then sees something and says to himself, 'that would look pretty good in a bouquet,' picks some and takes them to his florist to see what she thinks, then to another florist or two and then to a wholesaler and then, in a year or two, to a national floral distributor. That's the person who will end up with something successful."

As an example of that, he tells of the myrtle bushes that grow in the swamps all around southern Florida. "I have been walking around those bushes almost all my life, yet a young man I know came up with the idea that if he took all the leaves off those branches he could sell them to the silk flower people. They put silk foliage on them and they've got a wonderful looking branch. In the last four or five years he's established himself at this and I think he's probably selling a million dollars worth a year. But he worked at it and, most importantly, he saw it. That's what it takes."

Huffman thinks newcomers should concentrate on the decorative market. It's a very fragmented, widespread market with different possibilities all over the country, and with many, many different buyers with different needs. The large medicinal, pharmaceutical markets, on the other hand, are concentrated, and their suppliers are able to control things relatively easily—simply by lowering their prices enough to drive any newcomers out. The worldwide large pharmaceutical market for herbs is almost closed for newcomers, says Huffman, and he cites his own 25 year effort to get into it as evidence.

Saw palmetto berries grow with abandon along the roadsides of Florida. In the early Spanish days in that area, Marlin tells us, the local Indians used the berries for food and let the Spaniards know that during the harvest season the old Indians never had prostate trouble. The Spaniards, too, began to ingest the berries and, with the same results, took both the information and the berries back to Europe, where they have been used for centuries in the treatment of prostate inflammation.

The FDA, says Huffman, "has caused a lot of limitations to the possibilities of herbs in medicine in America. They issued a ban against using saw palmetto in the U.S. as a medicine and making any claims about it. I tracked down the man who issued that ban and asked him why he wrote the ban. First of all, he told me, that was none of my business. I called my senator and in about 20 minutes the FDA guy called back and begged me to talk to him. He then told me that the law provides that you have to prove its efficacy, to prove that it's not dangerous. The Europeans have been using this for 300 years, I reminded him.

"'But no one has ever proved that it works, or that it isn't dangerous.'

"Then I asked him if anyone, anywhere had ever been reported to have died or even been made sick from saw palmetto berries. He said no, not that he'd ever heard of. But what if they did, he asked, and I replied—and what if a star fell out of the heavens."

Proving that it works and/or isn't dangerous, is the madness here because, of course, such a study will cost over $200,000,000 and then the medicine itself cannot gain a patent—so no company who financed such a study could ever get their money back. What modern herbalists are asking is that the FDA accept the long tradition of medical herbalism in this country, just as Europe along with the rest of the world accepts it, and then to concentrate in a cooperative effort in studying and limiting the very few herbs for which there is even some hint of danger. So far that spirit of cooperation has not appeared. But appear it must, I believe, because herbalism has become so much of a grass roots practice now that the negative FDA efforts can only lead to greater and greater efforts on the part of a growing part of the population to learn ever more about plant-based medicines.

Meanwhile, Marlin tells us that most Caucasians consider the palmetto berry taste to be quite insipid. "It took me several years to develop a taste for them, but now they taste like money," he grins. For years his family gathered the berries along the roadsides and dried them on cement slabs here on the property we are on. Later, they could afford some "old rickety dryers," and a few years later began to buy from other wildcrafters (now numbering as many as 5000 people during harvesting season). Finally, they were able to put in the huge propane dryers they use now. The berries are stored in gunnysacks and shipped to Europe and all over the U.S.

At the time of our visit, the trucks were being loaded with red pepper berries, a wild roadside plant that Huffman ships to the decorative markets in the U. S. and Europe. Yes, he has heard some complaints from environmentalists about all the picking, which brings up some other theories he has about wildcrafting. "We pick just under 10 million pounds of these palmetto berries per year," says Huffman, "and that is approximately 1/10th of one per cent of what's out there. There is no way I could affect that species with the picking. But, of course, there are other species, like slipper orchids, for instance, where I could make a difference and those need to be protected. But the best place to start with the restrictions," he insists, "is with all those new roads going into the forests and all the habitat destruction."

This issue, along with the growing restrictions from the FDA, is slowly pushing the entire Huffman operation out of this country. Their other main crop, passionflower, contains a flavanoid that causes the human body to relax. It is used as a nervine all over Europe. Huffman has found that he can select from the wild and then cultivate plants that are much more concentrated in that property than what is found in the random content of wild plants. A few years ago the family purchased land in Guatemala where his son, Michael, now a permanent resident there, oversees the growing of passionflower and several other crops, some of which the family once grew in the U.S., or collected from the wild. Michael, who has degrees in horticultural production and agricultural economics from Purdue University, found land in Central America that can grow both tropical and subtropical plants very well. Soon almost the entire crop of saw palmetto berries will also be cultivated rather than picked from the wild.

The cost of living in the U.S. has now become so high, says Marlin, that wildcrafters must earn more money than the product itself can sometimes carry in the marketplace. Although his own office is shaded by trees covered with Spanish moss, he actually now imports this same moss from Mexico, and ships it to various foreign and domestic markets. "Pickers here have to make 75 or 80 dollars a day at that, while pickers in Mexico can live well on a quarter of that. And the product itself can't carry the higher price. It just won't sell."

A few years ago Marlin noticed that the dried flower market contained no miniature roses. As a test, they grew a hundred plants in Guatemala and sold the blossoms easily. They now have 80 acres down there in miniature roses. He looks constantly for little openings like that, where the market isn't already closed. On a recent trip to Holland he noticed a bouquet with a sea grape leaf in it. The source was Haiti where the leaves are dried on rooftops and often come to market with holes in them or chicken manure on them. Huffman came home and put in a little sea grape farm, and now sells a few semi-trailer loads of it a year.

This is the part of the business he loves, and would like to spend more of his time at now: checking out all the markets and then going out to look in the fields and woods, and along the shorelines, for new products, "cutting them off with my pocket knife, learning about them and trying to find a market, like I used to do. But this is such a big operation now that I just don't get the time any more." The phone rings constantly in the background as we talk. Huffman is wired in to a worldwide network and, as a supplier of botanicals on a large scale, he often gets phone calls from people out of the country looking for this or that product. If Huffman doesn't grow or collect it himself, he almost always knows just where to get it.

We walk through the rows of trial plants. Some are definitely off limits to visitors, and obviously contain plants the Huffmans are considering for the future. Some, like papayas the size of small watermelons, are very impressive indeed. But most impressive is Huffman himself, a true wildcrafter to his bones. He is remembering with great clarity the years spent trying to raise a family "in a little cracker shack up off the ground with no indoor plumbing," as he tried and tried to earn a living as a wildcrafter. Now he contemplates moving more and more of his company out of the country as it becomes a real part of the growing worldwide economy.

"What really made this company," he remembers, "is the accumulated knowledge over the years. Just being out there all the time and learning about everything. If you fail often enough at the same thing and never give up, sooner or later you can't help yourself—you'll make it. But you have to be like a fisherman," he says, "and learn where the fish are at. I am convinced you could throw me out anywhere in the world and in six months I would find something alongside the road you could sell."

I'm totally convinced of that myself.

But I am also convinced, as I think Marlin Huffman is, that more and more restrictions will soon apply to much of the open land in America. Stories like the ones this year of killings among the mushroom hunters only add to pressure already being put upon officials throughout the country where small armies of collectors often go into the woods in search of plants that bring high prices.

Writing in the May/June '93 issue of *The Business of Herbs*, herbalist Steven Foster lists several states where new laws to protect wild plants are coming into play, and also national forests where new plant removal restrictions now apply. I think I'll let his impressions be the final words on the subject of wildcrafting, as I think his words may well represent the future.

"Future impact from these developments (restrictions and fees on collecting from the wild) *is in the offing for the herb industry. Areas in which wild-harvesters can dig herbs may be limited in the future. This will cause a decreased supply, and coupled with user fees on federal lands, will increase the price of raw materials, perhaps substantially. The herb industry may also be perceived as the 'bad guys.' If the industry does not wake up to the inevitable, it is going to find itself short of raw materials and in a bad public relations position within less than five years.*

"Efforts must be developed to stimulate commercial cultivation, which includes the need for funding of basic research in propagation, cultivation, and other aspects of production."

Wildcrafting References

American Ginseng Trends Newsletter, published by Future Concepts. Bimonthly, for $28 from PO Box 1982, Wausau, WI 54402-1982. 715-675-4898.

Includes information on harvesting, pricing, marketing, and cultivation of ginseng.

Direct Marketing Directory: Ethical Wildcrafters and Organic Growers of Medicinal Herbs. Compiled by Rocky Mountain Herbalist Coalition, 412 Boulder St. Gold Hill, Boulder, CO 80302. $9.00 postpaid.

Seeing the Forest Instead of the Trees. To be published in 1994, from Midwest Research Institute, 425 Volker Blvd., Kansas City, MO 64110. 816-753-7600.

A series of technical assistance papers concerning making money collecting and selling forest products such as floral greenery, botanicals, and mushrooms. Contact the company for prices and availability. (Growing for Market)

Pacific Northwest Conference on Special Forest Products.

Scheduled for Spring 1994, this conference is for amateurs and professionals interested in special forest products: berries, mushrooms, ferns and floral greens, including plants which produce pharmaceuticals. The proceedings from the conference will be available in mid-year from Western Forestry and Conservation Association, 4033 SW Canyon Rd., Portland, OR 97221, Attn. Christy Dorsey. 503-266-4562. (HortIdeas)

The Wild Foods Forum. Twelve issues for $15 per year from 4 Carlisle Way NE, Atlanta, GA 30308. Sample copies are $1.50.

Good resource for both would-be wildcrafters and herbal teachers. Food foraging is fun, and this little newsletter helps to prove that. All about what's "out there" and how to use it.

WILDCRAFTING BUSINESSES

Native Scents. Al Savinelli, PO Box 5639, Taos, NM 87571

Plantation Botanicals. Marlin Huffman, PO Box 128, Felda, FL 33930

TEACH-ING ABOUT HERBS

One of the most appealing things about

teaching or selling information about herbs

is the wonderful effect it has on the person

doing the teaching or information selling.

Teaching About Herbs

Almost every single person we interviewed for this book has done some herbal teaching of one kind or another. Almost everyone I've ever known to be involved in herbs has been called upon to share their knowledge in one form or another, at least by speaking at the local garden or horticultural club, or giving a class at an herb farm. People who own and operate herb farms offer classes in everything from planting perennials to making wreaths. Nowadays there are even books published to help people give speeches or programs about herbs (see page 216).

The herbal renaissance this book is about is still so new in America that, if you are at all knowledgeable about herbs, you will be asked to share that knowledge with others in your community who are ever anxious to learn more about the useful plants. These next chapters are about different ways people turn that sharing of herbal knowledge into a separate small business effort.

When you are first learning to speak about herbs, chances are you won't want to charge for your time and effort—you'll probably just be glad for the opportunity to learn to do it well. But, as time goes by, and the invitations increase along with your ability to give a good program, you may want to consider charging a fee. At that point it's time to give some thought to the business possibilities that can be based on lots of good herbal knowledge.

If there is one business opportunity that everyone agrees represents today's ideal business, it would be the business of selling information. No product on the shelf is becoming outdated, no packaging is used to increase the size of the waste dumps, and relatively little pollution results from brain to brain business dealings. An added plus to an information business is that there is a constant, even daily opportunity to add new information, bring things up to date and provide an ever better information product. Now add in the positive fact that good teaching also carries a special potential—the possibility of actually helping to change someone's life for the better; that potential can be especially strong in teaching about herbs.

For me, one of the most appealing things about teaching or selling information about herbs is the wonderful effect it has on the person doing the teaching or information selling. To be successful at it, the teacher must keep up on the news about herbs and learn ever more about the possibilities for the useful plants of the world. Most of the people on the planet are dependent on these plants and just that knowledge keeps me tied, if only by a thin thread, to people all over the world. I follow medical news, agricultural news, environmental news, with a special interest that comes from a strong personal interest in all things herbal. All of it affects me, is a part of my life. A strong interest in herbs along with learning more and more information about herbs ties me snugly into the web of world life.

The following chapters, plus the reference section that follows them, offer a look at some of the potential in this field of herbal knowledge. I have also tried to list all the recommended herbal schools that people have told us about in our travels around the country, and to reference other possibilities about ways to teach about herbs. Teachers are unusual people. See if you recognize yourself in any of these portraits and if teaching about herbs could or should be a part of your business efforts.

Carole Tashel, Santa Fe

CAROLE TASHEL BEGAN her teaching career in the '70s, in classical piano. In the 1980s she began studying nutrition and natural foods cooking. She then spent a little time living in a Sufi community in New York, where she learned not only about Muslim mysticism, but about natural foods cooking and the subject of herbs. Carole is a slim, attractive young woman with incredibly large dark eyes that I thought might be those of an Egyptian genealogy. "No," she smiled. "Just Italian, and some Russian Jew in there, too.

"I must be a born teacher," she muses, "because I came home from that experience in New York, organized all their recipes, and put together a little class on natural foods cooking and herbs. I remember thinking that I had so much great information to share with people. I contacted the adult night school and the local parks and recreation district in Los Angeles, where I lived, about giving classes. I guess I've been teaching about herbs in one way or another ever since."

And she's also been learning more about herbs ever since, a typical pattern among all herbal teachers: their own learning never stops. Carole spent a couple of years with herbal instructors in the Los Angeles area and then decided she needed more formal training. She attended the Breitenbush Herbal Conference, a yearly Oregon get together of herbalists from around the country and, following that, took a month long apprenticeship program with Ed Smith, well known herbalist from the Herb Pharm, also in Oregon.

Michael Moore, founder of Herbs, Etc. in Santa Fe, had started his own program at the Institute for Traditional Medicine, in New Mexico, a school which offered an even more in-depth study of herbs. Carole went to learn from Michael Moore and was soon involved in the herbs of the Southwest, learning field work, pharmaceutical practices and medicine-making, right along with a strong training in anatomy, physiology, and therapeutic nutrition.

During that time of intensive learning, Carole continued teaching about herbs herself through several methods, one of which is her program of herbal walks, a program she continues to this day:

"When you join these local trips to the mountains, you'll delight in becoming acquainted with useful medicinal and edible plant friends you never realized were there! Your senses will awaken, you'll nibble on green things, tune into the earth in a new way, and learn things you'll never forget. "

The walks take place usually on weekend days, are from 9 AM to 3 PM, and cost $25 dollars, with children under 12 free, and a "sliding scale available if needed."

Her notices go up on bulletin boards around the town of Santa Fe, and she sends out notices to those she thinks will be interested. Tashel also teaches in other ways and, over time, has put together a list of herb enthusiasts from around the area.

The group, usually eight to 12 people, gathers at a central location to carpool to the walk site; they bring their own brown bag lunch and rain clothes. These are not really strenuous walks, says Carole, "it's more like an herbal mosey." That way she can encourage even 70-year-olds to come along and learn about the plants.

She begins the event with the participants seated on the ground in a circle, and a brief group sing to get everyone relaxed. Then she talks a few minutes about why what they are doing might be useful, and just what the personal pay-off might be for learning about wild medicinal plants. This always leads, she says, to a discussion of people taking more responsibility for their own health, and how that idea connects people to the earth and even to the idea of defending the land against abuse and overdevelopment. They get into "all sorts of issues beyond the purely personal," says Carole, long before they even look at a single plant.

When she does direct their attention to the plants around them, that little time spent in the circle relaxing and talking among themselves seems to help participants tune in on a deeper level, and that makes the rest of the teaching experience go very easily, she says. "The group has explored some important ideas before they actually begin to learn about specific plants."

One of Carole's greatest interests is in seeing the effect plants and flowers have on people, before any knowledge of the plant is given out. She will have her students focus on a wild plant, then give each one of them a leaf or flower from the plant. With their eyes closed, they pass the plant part over their body, smell, taste, touch it, and then tell what they think the plant might be used for, and how it affects them right there and then.

She is constantly surprised at the reactions people get from plants at this elementary level, and it is this interaction between plant and person that fascinates her and often influences her own learning path. She feels that as people open up their senses more, they are able to learn directly from the plants, "reactivating an ancient pathway of knowledge."

Carole Tashel's herbal walks begin with an informal discussion and a group sing.

On her walks, Tashel gives special attention to the most common plants, those that are usually seen only as "weeds," and takes great pleasure in teaching how these plants help heal the earth and how useful, even tasty, they can be. In early spring, for instance, the new shoots of nutritious tumbleweed are dug up to taste. "We have everything we need right here around us," says Carole who, like others we interviewed, tends not to be too carried away with exotic herbs from afar. With her long interest in cooking, she also spends considerable time talking about different ways to prepare herbs and local wild food. Sometimes she'll even bring along a small amount of salad base so the students can add bits of wild herbs to it and then enjoy the salad while on the outing.

Carole doesn't have people fill out any paperwork to take her walks, and hasn't increased her personal insurance, although she knows other herb leaders who do. Herbal walks are not her only means of teaching about herbs. She also gives classes through the Santa Fe Community College on The Healing Principles of Herbal Medicine, which is a five-week course with one evening class per week. She gives another class through the college called "Stalking The Wild Herbs," that is really much like her own herbal walks. She had no trouble getting started with the college doing herbal classes. "These classes aren't considered part of the academic program, and lots and lots of people want to take them. In fact, there's always a waiting list." She earns $150 per day for the herb walk classs, and 15 to 20 dollars per hour for teaching the five-week class.

At home, Carole teaches semi-private herbal apprenticeship programs, a 10-week, 40-hour program that gives a more in-depth study of medicinal herbs and their applications. This program is limited to eight students, and costs approximately $200. She also teaches classes on medicinal herbs in the summer program of the New Mexico Academy of Advanced Healing Arts. These are week-long, all-day classes for both lay people and massage therapists and other natural health practitioners. These classes cost about $350 per student.

Her tie-in with the New Mexico Academy gives Tashel lots of publicity because they do large mailings all around the state and even around the country. She also had a very part-time job (usually only one or two days a week for eight years) at Daniel Gagnon's herb shop, Herbs, Etc., in Santa Fe. She valued this retail experience because it kept her in touch with consumers and their attempts to heal themselves through the use of herbs. She got constant feedback from the store customers and kept careful notes on the effectiveness of the herbs. It is easy to see what a web of expertise she has built for herself as a teacher and always, always, as an ever more active learner.

Carole is able to support herself through this mixed teaching and working schedule and still maintain her own learning and interest in herbs. She travels occasionally and leads herbal walks in other parts of the country where she is able to spend a little time. She, too, feels caught up, as many modern herbalists do, in the current effort to create a new and more reputable sense of American herbalism. A unifying philosophy, she believes, is needed to bring together the long herbal traditions of the Native Americans and Hispanics, and the rich traditions of Europe— where so much American tradition actually comes from—and then to add in the ancient traditions of China and India. It is this all-encompassing understanding that American herbalists are looking for these days, and that people like Carole Tashel are strengthening in their own continuing efforts to teach all they can while always continuing to learn more themselves.

Kaye Cude, Florida

"WHEN WE RETIRED and moved to Florida, no one was growing and marketing herbs in the area, so it seemed like a great opportunity to do something I'd really enjoy. Very soon I found out why no one had been doing it." That's Kaye Cude of Buckingham, Florida, editor and publisher of *Spice and Herb Arts*, the newsletter for people who want to grow herbs and spices in hot, tropical areas. Her original idea of a market herb garden in the tropics proved to be a tough one.

"The hort and ag authorities just said to forget it—it couldn't be done." But Kaye and a few others decided to ignore that advice. At first, she says, "we had more failures than successes. This is definitely not an easy growing area. But now people look forward to buying the great plants that are produced here."

After Kaye registered the fictitious business name, Orange River Organic Spice-Herb Farm, in the local newspaper, she was inundated with people wanting her to come and teach about herbs and spices: libraries, local community colleges, shops—all wanting her to provide information they believed she must have. As she learned she began to teach.

After most of a lifetime of teaching, Kaye Cude is an innate, inveterate, incessant teacher. Whatever she learns, she simply has to pass on to others. She began publishing *Spice and Herb Arts* in 1987, and six times a year since then, she tells her subscribers everything she's learned about growing ginger, mangoes, allspice, bananas, water celery (*oenanthe javanica*), and lychees. All she's learned about temperate herbs and the substitutes for them that work in the tropics: *Tagetes lucida* for tarragon, *Lipia micromera* and *Coleus amboinicus* for oregano. Then there's Sago Palm cones for crafts, and scores of other exotica that people can grow and use when they live where the temperature seldom drops below 55°.

Her teaching only follows intensive learning on her own. Ordinary gardening methods, she says, just didn't work in her area. "We had to learn to grow in sand that requires lots of improvement before it can even qualify as poor soil."

She teaches how to grow in raised beds, and how to create them by first covering several layers of newspaper with several inches of mulch, followed by a layer of manure. She then scatters all-purpose fertilizer and a tiny amount of agricultural lime over that. Then ribbons of dish detergent are poured over, to act as a wetting agent. ("Now that's not dishwasher detergent," she says, patting my arm as I write.) A very few inches of good soil are then put on the top to complete this bed for growing in areas of very poor soil.

If you live in the tropics and want to grow plants, your problems are Kaye's problems and her journal supplies welcome information. Her small farm is on Muddy Lane in Buckingham, a few miles inland from Ft. Myers, Florida. *Musings from Muddy Lane,* the back page of the newsletter, is about life on her five acres and invites reader response.

Many other birds now inhabit the garden outside my office window, as do butterflies and pesky squirrels. After dark, bat-sized moths fly nearby and this year the fire-light or lightning bugs are back. Somewhere I once read that these bugs are able to ingest slugs after injecting the slug with an enzyme to dissolve it. Does anyone know?

In gardens where armadillos are one of the major pest problems, where temperate crop growing begins at the end of summer and does well in the middle of winter, where crops like pigeon peas need to be grown to actually shade summer crops, and where soil temperatures are often above 80°, many look to the teachings of Kaye Cude to help them become tropical gardeners.

They also get Kaye Cude, the retired teacher therapist (which means she taught teen-aged girls with behavior problems, in residential treatment centers), who digs up information on tropical plants and trees from all over the world and layers it in with classical reminders from Virgil, "*Praise be to those who learn to un-*

derstand nature's secrets and raise themselves above the need to rely on superstition," to Ecclesiastes, *"He hath made every thing beautiful in its time,"* which is the heading from the craft page.

In between come lots of ideas for crafting with herbs, unusual recipes for using all the tropical plants, plus a regular calendar of special places and events with the frequent admonition to GO AND LEARN!

Kaye also teaches around her area in libraries, botanical gardens, and community colleges. She advertises her newsletter

in the classes she gives, and advertises the classes in her newsletter. She calls the newsletter an "efficient way" to deal with both of her loves: plant knowledge and teaching. Importantly, it also allows her to keep her privacy. Visitors aren't allowed at the farm. "I don't have the required insurance or the personal time or energy to cope with people there and still do the things I love to do." She doesn't take questions on the telephone, but tries to deal with the more important ones in the journal.

She offers some cuttings, seeds, and plants to subscribers, and also in her workshops and classes, or at shops in the area. She also accepts a few ads in the newsletter: classified ads for ten dollars and a very few display ads. She asked for camera-ready copy for the ads to begin with, but "that didn't work out," so now she sets the ads herself on the computer. Most ads are for tropical plant nurseries, herb and craft shops, tropical fruit stores, or gift shops in Florida. She charges $12.50 for a year's subscription, six issues, and Florida residents must add an additional 75¢.

Kaye learned to use a word processor in order to put out the eight page 8½"x11" journal. She takes the camera-ready copy to

the printer, then picks it up when it's ready and carries it to the
post office. She uses a bulk rate permit and sends out over 700
copies. A friend, Melinda Copper, did the logo for the newsletter, which is an attractive line drawing of a three-inch wreath of
tropical herbs and fruits. Melinda also does some of the line
drawings in each issue.

Kaye's newsletter efforts are a tiny sample of a publishing/
communication phenomenon that has occurred in the country
in the last 20 years or so: namely, computer desktop publishing
and niche marketing.

Computers have turned every one of us into a would-be publisher, and niche marketing techniques offer us a way to reach
out and target those would-be readers whose interests are close
to our own. It seems a strange but very interesting phenomenon
that many American general interest magazines and newspapers
are in financial trouble these days, yet there are countless new
magazines and newsletters starting up monthly, even weekly.
Many of these are becoming quite successful by offering a much
more narrow, yet sometimes deeper layer of information to their
readers.

Kaye's journal is written primarily for a small geographic gardening area with distinctive gardening problems and differences
that don't quite fit into the endless supply of garden magazines
and books published each year across the land. Her readers follow along with her in their own tropical growing, network with
others in the area for even more information, and learn far more
about the subject of tropical plants than they could from reading
any general interest magazine or newspaper. *Women's Day* or even
Organic Gardening magazines might carry an article once each
year or so about growing ginger, but Kaye writes about it in detail, about all her experience growing and using it, in almost every issue.

Gardening newsletters like Kaye's are also successful because
they tap into lots of new information that is coming out all
around the world about gardening and herbs. She learns the
techniques needed to produce and use unusual plants by actually

growing and using them, she adds in reputable information she finds in her reading and, over time, her own readers feed her bits of information that she in turn can pass on to her other readers.

Kaye teaches more classes each year. She conducts workshops in other areas when she's able to fit the traveling into her schedule. She often helps friends and botanical gardens with herbal picnics. She also markets sauces and flavoring mixes made from tropical products.

Kaye says she knows she's making money "because my tax man says I'm doing fine." She does her own bookkeeping, which she dislikes, well enough to keep the tax man happy. Three hundred subscribers, she says, are what it takes to make a publication worthwhile. At seven hundred she feels comfortable. She admits she doesn't make a lot of money on the journal, or the classes, or any other single thing she does, but she's doing so many things in the way of teaching and learning that she can only be considered as happy and content. At the time of our visit, Kaye had just accepted an offer to market her herbs and products in a new specialty garden shop. Now she usually spends a couple of days each week there and also teaches classes in the shop. She's considering taking a few months off from the newsletter in order to finish a book she's started and reorganize some activities. For a **retired** person she is truly amazing.

Kaye shares her recipes on the *Days of Plenty* page of *Spice and Herb Arts.* Her mustard sauce is splendid and, with her permission, I'll pass it along.

Kaye Cude Mustard Sauce

Yield 6+ cups.

2 cups pureed onion

¼ cup pureed fresh ginger root

½ teaspoon ground allspice or
2 large allspice leaves (remove midvein)

½ teaspoon anise extract or
1 tablespoon fresh tarragon leaves

12 orange mint leaves

1 tablespoon herb vinegar

1 quart yellow mustard

1 hot pepper (optional)

Put above ingredients in food processor and mix
until well blended. Store in refrigerator.

Herbal Bed & Breakfast, British Columbia

ONE OF MY most pleasant herbal learning experiences came last year on a visit to a little bed and breakfast on beautiful Mayne Island, in the Canadian Gulf Islands. My teachers were Judith Solie-Engelhardt and her husband, Jürgen, owners of the Tinkerer's Retreat, a small, well kept, rustic lodge along the shores of Active Pass.

Like so many other herbalists met along the path of this book, Judy and Jürgen are unusual, interesting, even passionate teachers. Jürgen specializes in teaching people to take charge of their lives, and also to learn the traditional art of tool sharpening; Judy teaches herbal workshops specializing in an intensive introduction to herbal medicine and body knowledge. They have developed a unique approach which blends together the practical and intuitive, along with some theoretical and more scholarly information.

They spend their summers on the small remote island between Vancouver Island and mainland Canada, keeping their house full of guests and students who come to learn from two strong voices for independence and self-care. Jürgen and Judy are also tied in with many other people and activities in Mexico and Europe, where they travel for part of every year.

The house itself can sleep about 10 or 12 extra people, with a small outbuilding housing a dining hall and extra showers. The windows of the lodge face out on one of the most incredible waterways in the northwest: Active Pass is the seaway for millions of salmon returning each year to the waters of the Fraser River in Canada (and therefore patrolled by all the fishermen of the area and beyond) and also the passageway for the endless ferryboats that run between Vancouver, the largest city in the province of British Columbia, and Victoria, the capital of that province. Visually the area is stunning, and the house itself is surrounded by large, varied herb and vegetable gardens that provide much of the food and some of the livelihood for the Engelhardts.

Their herbal workshops are held over a Saturday and Sunday and include a Saturday lunch and dinner and a Sunday breakfast, with plenty of learning activities in between the delicious herb-based meals. The cost was 75 dollars per person. As a student, I felt that I got my money's worth, and then some.

This is not easy earning for the Engelhardts. They don't hire

The Tinkerer's Retreat is a small, well-kept, rustic lodge on Mayne Island in the Canadian Gulf Islands

any extra help, so they are responsible for all the cooking, all the preparation and cleaning up for 10 or 12 guests and, of course, all the teaching. But they can take in $800 or $900 in less than two days and know that they've done an excellent job in passing along their own enthusiasm for the healthful herbs.

The workshop began with a delightful lunch at noon on Saturday. The soup, the bread, the cheese spread, the tea, the salad dressing, the fruit sauce, all were incredibly well flavored with herbs, and all served family style in the little dining hall where everyone gets acquainted and relaxes over a delicious meal. My classmates included a few retired people, both American and Canadian, a practicing midwife from Victoria, a young Canadian doctor (a GP with a practice in Vancouver), and a couple of avid gardeners from other islands who wanted to learn more about growing and using medicinal herbs.

After lunch, we all gathered in the garden where Judy and Jürgen each took half the guests on a long, detailed trip through the gardens where the real teaching began. These are very focused gardeners whose gardens are also left alone for months at a time every year, and who seldom have to weed because of their intelligent, careful gardening techniques. The garden trip also reveals their strong attachment to the wild plants of the area—the plants most of us call weeds and that the Engelhardts (and so many other herbalists) call some of the most important plants of the world: sheep sorrel, lamb's quarters, plantain, shepherd's purse, dandelion, and nettles.

When they first began seriously learning about growing herbs, the Engelhardts say that they were put off by the same system they felt they saw in the herbal world as they had seen in the orthodox world of medicine—a disease approach that says that if you get this problem, you solve it with this herb. Instead, they have chosen to combine their interest in medicinal herbs with their strong interest in more ordinary wild plants, and to incorporate the two in their own approach to teaching about herbs. They do give detailed information about single herbs and their powers, but they mostly emphasize a preventive approach to health that includes the daily use of wild plants and herbs mixed in something the Engelhardts constantly refer to as their Herb Shake. More about that in a moment.

As far as the wild plants and weeds are concerned, the Engelhardts are very much in tune with much of modern herbalism about this. Most herbal references in the popular media are to specific, often powerful plants: ginseng, echinacea, goldenseal, etc., but much of the actual teaching of modern herbalism is about plant combinations and, most especially, about the use of these more common plants that are underfoot in our everyday lives. Most herbalists seem much more comfortable with the idea of prevention through a healthy diet and use of the green pharmacy—the one that's out there all around us. Build up our systems with those plants, they say, rather than taking up the constant search for **just the right powerful herb** for such and such a disease. That is too much like the *silver bullet* approach of allopathic (usual) medicine, they believe.

Judy did her Ph.D. thesis on the study of the wild medicinal plants of the northern hemisphere, using a systems approach to the body to organize the information about medicinal herbs. Nowadays, she and Jürgen travel every winter to Mexico to study the wild plants of that area. "We take folkloric information on these plants and look to see if there is scientific information to back it up." Both come from strong herbal traditions in Europe: Jürgen was born in Germany, Judy is second generation Norwegian.

"My mother survived World War II in Europe living on wild plants. When times are unstable, questionable, difficult, I can look down onto the ground of the earth and it's all food to me," says Jürgen.

They came up with the idea for their Herb Shake years ago after first learning about the high nutritional value of herbs and wild plants from reading the well known cookbook, *Laurel's Kitchen*. They were living a traveling life style at the time, with no refrigerator or other usual means of storage. Jürgen built drying racks, found a kitchen blender that could run off a generator and, together, they came up with the idea for an Herb Shake, a blend of dried herbs that they could put together from the abundance of wild edible and medicinal herbs all around them. Both stress the importance of learning to combine culinary and medicinal herbs with wild edibles, and combining all of these with good, simple food for good nutrition.

The Engelhardts are very skilled at this system of preparing simple, flavorful food, which means they were able to feed us very well at a relatively small expense to themselves, thus mak-

ing their income from the workshops even more valuable. It is
also clear that they have thought a great deal about just how to
handle guests and meals in such a way that they can also do the
teaching, and still seem relaxed and comfortable with a dozen
strangers prowling about the place, asking questions, picking
herbs, wandering off, wanting this, that, or the other.

After a delicious dinner of pasta, salad, and fruity drinks, we
gather in the main living room of the lodge and Judy begins the
more serious part of the workshop: trying to get people to be a
little more familiar with how their bodies work and just which
processes herbal medicines can affect.

She begins with coloring books that show the lymphatic system. Having learned that black and white text-like books can
really put people off, Judy finds that coloring books and bright
felt tip pens help people learn and more easily begin to understand bodily parts and processes. Then she hands out a bibliography, most of which is for books she has there to show her
students. Besides getting people oriented to the plants and the
human body, she wants to get them turned on to good reference
books.

Judy then starts with the cellular components of the lymph
system, how the blood travels through the system, the constant
filtering necessary—therefore, the importance of the liver, and
the work of the "T" cells, and other white blood cells.

"Think of it as a vast, floating armada," she says, "committed
to defending the self against anything perceived as non-self, with
a memory for any and all previous enemies, and also the capacity
to recognize and mark any as yet unknown intruders." One of
the most exciting dimensions of the immune system she tells us,
"is its ability to communicate with the nervous system and thus
influence and be influenced by our feelings." Judy spends lots of
time on the cellular components of the immune system, relating
them to herbs like echinacea and always touting their own use,
daily, of a dry mix made from the wild plants they believe to be
both medicinal and culinary.

Herb Shake

You must dry enough of the following greens to end up with about one cup full of herbs that have been dried and put through the blender. The contents may vary a bit, but nettles, the Engelhardts believe, are a must, both for flavor and for health.

Basil (*Ocimum basilicum*)
Bedstraw (*Galium spp.*)
Chickweed (*Stellaria spp.*)
Dandelion leaves (*Taraxacum officinale*)
Lamb's quarter (*Chenopodium album*)
Marsh violet (*Viola odorata*)
Miner's lettuce (*Montia spp.*)
Nettles (*Urtica spp.*)
Oregano (*Origanum spp.*)
Parsley (*Petroselinum crispum*)
Plantain (*Plantago spp.*)
Sheep sorrel (*Rumex Acetosella*)
Shepherd's purse (*Capsella bursa-pastoris*)
Thyme (*Thymus vulgaris*)

To this cup of dried, blended herbs, add 1 or 2 teaspoons of garlic, cayenne, and kelp powders, depending on taste; 1 or 2 tablespoons of soy lecithin, and then add powdered brewer's yeast to make a total of 2 cups of herb shake.

Nettles, they believe, are the most important ingredient for this Herb Shake, plus the addition of some of the following: plantain, dandelion, nasturtium, bedstraw, kelp, lamb's quarters, chickweed, miner's lettuce, sheep sorrel, and shepherd's purse. They dry these plants on screens installed along the kitchen ceiling and then, after a few days when the plants are dry, put them in a kitchen blender. They add brewer's yeast, garlic, and cayenne pepper for flavor and end up with a basic seasoning for food, and their own immune system enhancer. One coffee can full lasts them all winter added to soups, refried beans, oatmeal, and brown rice. They also shake it on popcorn, and add it to cream cheese to spread on toast. They have used it in our meals; I can guarantee how flavorful it is.

The Engelhardts also show us the other home remedies they make: from elderflower capsules to echinacea tinctures. Judy sits on the floor in the center, with all of us seated around the room—everyone comfortable, interrupting as we care to, and learning the bits and pieces most important to us. We have not only learned about the plants and gardening, but simple home remedies and how to make them, and a special recipe for something we've already tasted and found delicious. It is obvious that everyone feels they are certainly getting their money's worth in this workshop.

The following morning, after another tasty meal, the Engelhardts deal with questions from everyone. We've all slept on yesterday's information—now what do we need clarified? There's also a social side to the time spent: people getting acquainted, sharing experiences, while also comparing notes about herbs and herbal medicine. The Engelhardts are experts about their own island and those nearby as well, and gladly share travel tips with anyone wanting to see more of the area. Everyone takes their leave before lunch.

The herb weekends are only a small part of what the Engelhardts do to keep their lives and travels full and interesting. In the early '70s they took a boat, plus kayaks, from the Maritimes to Florida, outfitting the boat as a tool sharpening business, and calling themselves The Tinkerers. They then traveled all over North America in a similarly outfitted van, learning Spanish, teaching about herbs, plants, tool sharpening, and wilderness travel.

Their Mayne Island lodge is used yearly in the spring for Elderhostel workshops, and the Engelhardts also make unusual tours each year to Germany and Mexico. Currently under construction is the Tinkerer's Mayne Hostel, a 16 bed International Hostel, due to open in the summer of 1995. An ongoing feature of the hostel will be lecture demonstrations.

"The Tinkerers act as guides to anyone wanting to join them on their yearly journey; to sample their version of the time-honoured, nomadic way of life," reads their brochure. But in all they do, in each place they visit, herbs and wild plants are a part of their life and a big part of all their teaching.

Teaching References & Resources

BOOKS ON HERBAL TEACHING

The Art & Skill of Teaching About Herbs, by Portia Meares. Available for $18.95 + p&h, from Northwind Farm, Rt. 2, Shevlin, MN 56676.

A well known herbalist provides how-to-do-it herbal teaching information, plus copyright-free additions to use as reference material These can be used in promotions, or to photocopy for handout sheets in your classes.

Speaking of Herbs, by Betty Wold 15.95 postpaid from Rt 1, Box 80, Gore, OK 74434.

Ten introductory programs for speakers, including the talks, handouts that can be copied for the audience, and notes to the speaker about how to prepare for each program. Inviting and thorough. A nationally known writer and speaker, with this book Wold makes it easy to agree to be a public speaker about herbs in your community.

FILMS, SLIDE SHOWS, AUDIO & VIDEO TAPES

Herb Society of America, Inc., 9019 Kirtland-Chardon Road, Mentor, OH 44060. 216-256-0514.

A membership group, "not medically oriented," formed in 1933 for the purpose of "furthering the knowledge and use of herbs..." They sponsor research and tours, help establish public herb gardens, review lots of herb books and also offer **herbal slide shows for rent.** You must be recommended or sponsored in as a member. They do a lot of work on public herb gardens around the country.

Herbal Videos by Debra Nuzzi, M. H. Morningstar Publications, 177 Brook Circle, Boulder, CO 80302.

The Seeker Press, PO Box 2899, West Lafayette, IN 47906. 317-497-9381.

Large selection of herbal videos.

Goosefoot Acres Center for Wild Vegetable Research and Education, PO Box 18016, Cleveland, OH 44118. Tel & FAX 216-932-2145. Dr. Peter A. Gail, Director.

If you read *The Business of Herbs*, you've seen his entertaining columns on edible wild foods. He also does workshops, slideshows, etc.

Laura Clavio, 3014 No. 400 W., West Lafayette, IN 47906-5231.

Ms. Clavio reviews herbal videos for *The Business of Herbs*, and offers her previous reviews at a small cost: in the July '93 issue, she offered all previous herb video reviews for only $3. An excellent source for learning just which videos to offer in your own classes.

Tree Farm Communications, 23703 NE 4th St., Redmond, WA 98053. 800-468-0464. FAX 206-868-2495.

Large selection of video and audio tapes from herb conferences and seminars. Send for their brochure.

Wise Woman Herbals, PO Box 328, Gladstone, OR 97027.

Producers of a highly recommended video, **Edible and Medicinal Herbs.** Shows an herb walk in Oregon by a naturopathic pharmacist for the College of Naturopathic Medicine in Portland.

RECOMMENDED HERBAL SCHOOLS

California School of Herbal Studies, Amanda McQuade Crawford. 707-887-7457. Also sponsors the yearly Breitenbush Conference.

Rocky Mountain Center for Botanical Studies, 1705 14th St. #287, Boulder, CO. 80302. 303-442-2215.

New Mexico Academy of Healing Arts, PO Box 932, Santa Fe, NM 87504. 505-982-6271.

Jeanne Rose Herbal Studies Course by Correspondence, 219 Carl St., San Francisco, CA 94117. 415-564-6337. FAX 415-564-6799.

Clarissa Smith, Herbalist. PO Box 874, Wilson, WY 83014. 307-733-6811.

Bastyr College, 144 NE 54th St. Seattle, WA 98105. FAX 206-527-4763.

East West Master Course in Herbology. Correspondence. PO Box 712, Santa Cruz, CA 95061.

Dominion Herbal College, 7527 Kingsway, Burnaby, BC, Canada V0N 3C1.

Therapeutic Herbalism, 9304 Springhill School Rd., Sebastopol, CA 95472.

The Science and Art of Herbology. Box 420, East Barre, VT 05649.

The School of Natural Healing, PO Box 412, Springville, UT 84663. 801-489-4254.

TEACHING BUSINESSES

Carole Tashel. 6 Gavilan Pl., Santa Fe, NM 87505

Spice & Herb Arts. Kaye Cude, 5091 Muddy Lane, Buckingham, FL 33905

The Tinkerers. Jürgen and Judith Solie-Engelhardt, Box 83, Georgina Pt. Rd., Mayne Island, British Columbia, Canada V0N 2J0

RECOMMENDED BOOKS

Just Weeds, by Pamela Jones. Prentice Hall, 1991.

A true weed, she tells us, must be totally useless. Then come the details about thirty common "weeds" and their great usefulness. A fine introduction to turning your mind towards a true definition of weeds. She urges that we all become knowledgeable about weeds so that they become a normal part of life, like air and water and sun and earth. The book teaches us to learn to prepare these plants as foods, to use them in home remedies and cosmetics, to appreciate them as we do the better known herbs.

A Consumer's Guide to Alternative Medicine, by Kurt Butler, Prometheus Books, Amherst, NY, 1992.

If you are going to teach about herbs, or if you have an interest in medicinal herbs, here is a book to read and see if it knocks you off the path you have chosen. A strong attack on all "alternative" medicine and medical practices: if it doesn't come from a chemical laboratory or isn't written up on a prescription pad, it's bound to be snake oil. Acupuncture, Butler claims, teaches both ancient and modern "quackery." He also makes grand attacks on Transcendental Meditation, Christian Scientists, Naturopathy and a host of other "evils." Here is mainstream medicine with a vengeance. Read it to prepare yourself for skepticism about the world of herbs.

WRITING ABOUT HERBS

If cooking with herbs is your main interest, a cookbook could be in your plans. If herb gardening is your passion, or herb crafts, or herbal lore, you may want to pass along your herbal knowledge by writing magazine or newspaper articles or by book writing. For magazine writing, you need to consult a current issue of *Writer's Market*.

There are two primary roads to publication: one is to get a publisher, the other is to become your own publisher, which means to write the cookbook, and then publish it yourself. And self-publishing means hiring out or doing yourself all the steps in book manufacturing and book selling: the editing, typesetting, art work or photography, book design and book printing, followed by the *book selling* (a very involved and fairly complicated process that can take even more time and energy than the book writing itself.) The following resources should be of help if any of this is of interest to you.

Book Publishing References

How To Get Happily Published, by Judith Appelbaum. Harper & Row, 3rd edition. 1988.

Such a splendid, helpful book. An overview of the publishing picture and how you may fit into it. She writes from many years of working in the heart of the mainstream publishing world, yet brings great enthusiasm and a real sense of possibilities for newcomers to that world. Reading Applebaum is like having a long series of doors opened up. Upbeat, helpful, and reputedly very realistic about publishing possibilities. A good book to start with if publishing interests you.

How To Write A Cookbook and Get It Published, by Sara Pitzer. Writer's Digest Books, 1984.

A cookbook author with extensive publishing experience writes a friendly, even fascinating book on the overview and then the details, details, details, of publishing your own cookbook. A very thorough treatment—I can't imagine a better one.

The Complete Guide To Self-Publishing, by Tom & Marilyn Ross. Writer's Digest Books, 2nd edition, 1989.

Only a small part of a chapter on cookbook publishing, but a very interesting, easy-to-understand approach to book self-publishing. I have referred to this book, and the one that follows, very often over recent years and find them both very helpful.

The Self-Publishing Manual, by Dan Poynter. Para Publishing, 1984.

The original, complete bible of the self-publishing industry. Densely packed with an incredible amount of information on how to get into book publishing and marketing, written by a man who has been doing it with great success for a long time.

Is There A Book Inside You? by Daniel Poynter and Mindy Bingham. Para Publishing, Santa Barbara, 1992.

This is actually a book about getting organized to write a book, and then doing it. Practical, straight-ahead, full-speed, hands-on and very can-do. Makes you want to stop hesitating and get on with it.

WRITING, NEWSLETTER & BROCHURE HELP

Wheeler Arts, 66 Lake Park, Champaign, IL 61821-7101. 217-359-6816. FAX 217-359-8716.

Computer art for both PCs and Macs featuring lots of horticultural possibilities, including a disc of 55 herbal images.

Editing Your Newsletter, by Mark Beach. Coast to Coast Books, Portland, OR, 1988.

A very detailed approach from first planning to final distribution of a newsletter. A good basic reference. Lots of details for beginners. Can also be used by those without a computer. Paste-up, graphics, etc. A good introduction to design, printing, and layout.

Marketing With Newsletters, by Elaine Floyd. EF Communications, New Orleans, 1991.

A much more promotion and marketing oriented book than the previous one, this book is for people who are really serious about making a newsletter pay off. Offers tough, hard-hitting advice for anyone who needs to communicate very effectively with others in a limited time and space. Written completely from the newsletter reader's point of view. How to hook them and hold them. Written especially for promotional newsletters, this book should also help any writer design a better, easier-to-read newsletter.

Garden Writing: For Newsletters & Magazines, by Bob Gordon. Available for $8.95 + s&h, from Northwind Farms, Rt 2, Box 246, Shevlin MN 56676.

For beginning writers who have a lot of horticulture experience but not much writing experience.

OTHER POSSIBIL-ITIES

We are definitely living in the age of

small business, so the possibilities

seem almost endless.

Other Herb Business Possibilities

There are ever more small business opportunities in herbs—probably some of which I haven't heard or thought of. These plants and the interest in them have been around for a long, long time and we are definitely living in the age of small business, so the possibilities seem almost endless.

What follows are some bare outlines of other business possibilities that may spur your imagination and interest, a few leads to follow, and a hope on my part that readers will let me know of still other small herb business possibilities that might be included in any revised editions of this book. The herbal network in this country is already strong; I want this book to be a helpful addition to that information web.

More Herb Products

THERE ARE MANY, many other herbal products to consider—just not enough room in this one book to write about all of them. But here's a short list of other herbal products you might want to think about.

DRIED HERBS. When I first started selling green cut herbs more than ten years ago, I considered dried herbs not worth bothering with, other than those I dried in a little food dryer for my own kitchen. This last holiday season, while cooking at a friend's house, I needed a few dried sage leaves. The tiny jar was selling at the market at the rate of $365.83 per pound! I have since reconsidered my original thinking on this subject. Not only have the prices of dried herbs gone through the kitchen ceiling, but more and more people have learned that most dried herbs are fumigated, probably even nuked with radiation to kill the bugs. Many cooks now also realize that fresh dried is better than old dried—as in sitting on our kitchen shelves too long. Therefore, why not a little hanging cardboard display right near the jars of herbs in your market with tiny cellophane or plastic bags of dried herbs—just enough to prepare a few meals? Make sure the display says locally grown and organically grown. I think it would be an excellent seller. I'm sure enterprising herbalists must already be doing this around the country; I just haven't seen it in my area.

HERBAL JELLIES. Here's one I tried myself when I first started selling potted plants at the local farmers' market and then later at the Pike Place Market in Seattle. I still think it has great possibilities but, unlike the popular red and green pepper jellies, herbal jellies take real time and effort to work out recipes that give them true herbal flavors, rather than just a sweet taste. Selling them at farmers' markets means letting people taste them, and that can lead to a problem with the health department (about serving food on the street without the proper licensing, etc). I got so busy with other things that I simply gave up on the jellies but, just as with the dried herbs, people now seem willing to pay much more for fancy jams and jellies, so I think this herbal jelly idea is one worth considering. If you have wild berries in your area, perhaps these can be incorporated in a product line with the herb flavors. And give some thought to special labeling for local bed and breakfasts (who serve lots of jellies and jams) and who might want to offer your jellies to their guests.

HERBAL SEASONINGS. Best selling food items these days are mixed herbal seasonings that cooks can add to all sorts of dishes. I am thinking now about something in a special little packet (not just the resealable poly bags) that might have a local angle, perhaps to season a local specialty. In my area that would be salmon: special herbs to season grilled salmon, sold perhaps in a little cardboard fish-shaped packet that would sell to locals and tourists alike. What's special in your area? Corn, lobster, potatoes, sweet onions? Herb seasoning packets can be made up to go with any of those or a dozen others.

HERBAL CREAMS AND OILS. I think there is an unlimited market for herbal items like these in the cosmetic, bath, or skin product areas. An herb grower in my region developed a fine hand cream from calendulas (primarily) and I now see it offered in fancy mail order catalogs across the land.

HERBAL GREETING CARDS

HERBAL SOAPS

HERBAL PET PRODUCTS

FRAGRANCE BEADS

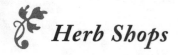

Herb Shops

ALMOST ALL HERB Farms have small (sometimes even large) shops associated with them, and it's time to say a few words about stand-alone herb shops, not connected with an Herb Farm or wholesale business. These are beginning to appear all around the country, especially in urban areas. Steven Foster, well known author and herbalist, sees the possibility of herb shops becoming a part of the retail scene in almost any town in America. "I can imagine," he said, "almost any community in the country being able to support such a shop before too long, so strong is the herbal renaissance becoming in America."

There are many important things to consider in opening and operating such a shop, the most important of which must be: location, financing, and a strong awareness of just what's involved in running such an operation. There are countless books and bulletins available for those looking to open a retail operation. What follows are just a couple of ideas I would like you to be sure and think about as you begin any serious consideration of such a business. These ideas stand out as important in my mind, as I look back at opening and operating three retail shops in the past.

TIME AND SPACE: Opening a successful retail shop is a very large time commitment. Over the years, I have noticed how many retail operators fail to understand this idea when they first decide to open a shop. Successful shops have **very regular** business hours and are **open at least part of every weekend**, so that other working people can find time to shop there. If you have a nine to five job now, with weekends off, you need to imagine working much longer hours than that in your own shop, at least for the first year or two—maybe even longer. The financial rewards in retailing are not quick rewards. And the primary rewards of owning your own small business—like mental freedom and the challenge to do the best possible job you can imagine—only seem to come to those who can pay the price in time and commitment. You cannot expect to work less than you probably do now, once you open your own business. Rather, be prepared for much more work, at least to begin with.

Unless you have unlimited funds, you are going to be the shop designer and display artist, goods buyer, bookkeeper and accountant, publicist, freight clerk and (most importantly) **store clerk** for quite a while when your shop first opens. In fact, you must continue with all those jobs until the shop becomes successful enough to support both you and other employees—which means carrying the added responsibility, not only for their salary, but unemployment insurance, plus other state and federal taxes, etc. Of course, this kind of involvement means you learn everything at a hands-on, very practical level and that you can ever afterward know from your own experience what any employees you hire should be doing—and you can also fill in when they cannot come.

You're also probably going to have to do all this solo stuff in a very small space—maybe just a few hundred square feet. Please try and think, at least a little bit, about the idea that shop keeping can be a real lock-up, both mentally and physically. One of the more positive things about owning and operating your own small shop is the opportunity it offers for making and remaking your own public environment: acting out those ideas you have about what kind of service and environment shops should provide to the buying public. But you must also remember that whatever environment you create, you could well be stuck in it yourself, day in and day out, for a long time to come. Keepers of small shops often go stir-crazy.

SHOPLIFTING: If I had to point to one thing that drove me out of retailing it would probably be shoplifting, that plague on the retail landscape that is seldom talked about but that every retail operator learns to dread. And not just because of the lost profits, which are certainly real enough, but because of what it does to your head. When shoplifting becomes a problem in your store, you begin not trusting the people who walk in the front door to shop (or rob) there. And when that happens your happy shop keeping days may well be numbered. For some people it can be just another, though difficult, part of the retail game. For others it is such a drag on the psyche that they, as I did, simply have to get out of the business. It is definitely something to think seriously about before you take the first steps in retailing. When you walk through shopping centers these days and wonder, for the hundredth time, just how on earth "they" can charge such outrageous prices for their goods, at least a part of the answer to that question lies in the problem of shoplifting, both by customers and by employees. It is a very big problem—probably far larger than you would ever imagine.

As far as getting good information on opening an herb shop, I would first concentrate on getting good business information from the library, from the Small Business Administration, from your banker, from your local college—there is a ton of this kind of straightforward small business info available, and you need to read lots of it to get a feel for what you are getting into. Much of it may be boring, much may not really relate, but it is a kind of a learning process that will help you have a little self-confidence when you start. At least you know what the lingo is about.

Find out what licenses you need to operate in your area. Learn how the retail credit system operates, what kind of terms and discounts you can expect in your purchases, what kind of credit services you can offer your own customers. Read about how to find a good retail location, how to deal with landlords about a lease, how to write a business proposal, and how to put all your ideas on paper, so that you can convince bankers and others to help you when and if you need help. Try to estimate how much cash it will take you to operate comfortably until you can begin making a profit.

And then start checking out the channels for getting good information on herbal products. Many of these channels are mentioned in the previous reference sections. Subscribe right away to at least *The Business of Herbs* and whatever other trade magazines you can afford. Attend herb fests and herb conferences in your area, visit herb farms and any other herb shops in your vicinity. Visit at least one major gift show to get an idea of just how much stuff is "out there"—products that you can offer in your shop.

Use the Herb Resource Directories listed in the previous reference sections and write postcards to herb companies around the country that sound like they might have something of interest for your shop. Get your own information network going so that you can start getting the knowledge you need to run a smart, successful business. What skills can you develop so that you can also teach classes at your shop? What seminars can you sponsor to keep spreading the word on herbs in your area? Start thinking of your store as a little information headquarters in your neighborhood or region, where people can come and learn more about the usefulness of herbs. People want to buy products where they get good service, and providing reliable information is, in my opinion, just about the best service you can offer your customers.

HERB SHOP REFERENCES

Small Business Administration (SBA) 409 Third St., SW, Washington, DC 20024. 1-800-368-5855.

This government agency, set up to help finance and assist small businesses, is primarily an information center. They offer a list of publications on pricing, mail order, home-based business, etc. (at SBA Publications, PO Box 1000, Ft. Worth, TX 76119) and videotapes on how to start and manage a successful small business, plus pre-business training workshops, and some management counseling provided by (usually) retired business people. There are also district offices of the SBA in many areas.

How To Write A Business Plan, by Mike McKeever. Nolo Press, Berkeley, CA, Revised Edition, 1988.

The real subject is money for a business, and how to get it. Cash flow analysis, profit and loss forecasts, all those eye glazing subjects you know you ought to learn about but can't really bear to think about.

McKeever makes it a little easier and even offers to critique his readers' business plans—for the price of a lunch. But his serious offer is to help you think through and put down on paper a complete business plan designed to help you raise the money to finance your business and, even more importantly, to help you think through the validity of the business idea itself, your suitability for it, and its chances for survival. If everyone who intended to do a small business would read this book and do the homework he recommends, there would probably be far fewer small business failures, and very probably, far fewer small businesses. He's not that discouraging, just very realistic.

Growing A Business, by Paul Hawken. Simon & Schuster, NY, 1987.

A perfect opportunity to recommend, again, this splendid little book about opening up and growing a business. If you are considering any business, read both Hawken and McKeever (above). They will help you do a splendid job.

Herb Restaurants

BY NOW YOU may well have heard of The Herbfarm restaurant here in the Pacific Northwest, just south of Seattle. It's had many write-ups and reviews for its fabulous food, but almost as many newspaper pieces about its ability to draw a seemingly endless supply of lunch and dinner guests at prices way above average: the luncheons are $45, and dinners run just over a hundred dollars per person.

Spring and summer reservations are taken on a certain day, usually in early April. Fall and holiday reservations are taken on a day in August. On those days the phone lines to the restaurant number simply jam up, and all reservations are quickly taken. Recently they have started leaving a quarter of all seats unbooked, and those are offered by telephone every Friday at 1 PM for the following week. This restaurant is not known for its empty seats. Ever.

What's going on here? Well, delicious food for one thing. Surrounded by seventeen herb gardens and a relatively small herb shop, The Herbfarm restaurant is one of many around the country that have proved how eager many people are for the unusual in flavor and menu.

Duo of Miniature Northwest Cheese Souffles With Jerusalem Artichoke and Beet Chips; Medley of Basil-Wood-Smoked Seafoods Wrapped in Garden Greens With Fresh Seaweed and a Carrot Sauce; Three-tree Sorbets; Herb-Crusted Supreme of Pheasant With a Green Walnut Wine Sauce; A Salad From Our Gardens; Warm Carmel-and-Sage-Baked Pear Tart With a Homemade Soft Cheese and Fresh Bay Filling On Apricot and Cranberry Custard Sauces; Rosemary-Walnut Bread; Calendula-Flower Butter—these are serious six course luncheons and nine course dinners with wines—plus guided tours in the gardens. In other words, events.

"You'll begin with a hosted garden tour, then move indoors for the orchestrated three-hour meal. Because each course is chosen by chef Jerry Traunfeld—and because The Herbfarm serves just one seating most Fridays, Saturdays, & Sundays—great care can be focused on each meal."

In Mason, New Hampshire, near the border with Massachusetts, out Route 31, take a right at the blinking light just past the turn off to Greenville, up a winding road to Nutting Hill Road, and then, welcome to Pickity Place, a restaurant, herb garden, shop and book store located in and around a 200-year-old house that once inspired the illustrations for the 1948 version of Little Red Riding Hood.

This herb restaurant opens every day for three seatings for lunch: that's about one hundred people a day who enjoy a five-course meal for $12.95 plus tax. On our visit, the meal began with Bacon Horseradish Dip (which is also sold in the shop), a small bowl of Mushroom Barley Soup, Sweet Corn Muffins, a September Salad of cucumbers, tomatoes, and lettuce with a cheese herb dressing, an entree choice of Baked Fish with Garlic, Basil and Tomatoes, or Vegetable Stroganoff with lots of vegetables in a light creamy sauce over green noodles. The vegetables were Brussels Sprouts with Poppy Seeds and Sherry, and dessert was Pumpkin Cheese Cake with Kahlua Glaze, plus herbal teas, hot or iced.

Almost everyone visited the book shop or herb and gift shop before or after lunch. Judy and Dave Walter have been running Pickity Place for almost fifteen years, and their dining room help is remarkably friendly and helpful, even through the third serving, which was our choice. They advertise a lot in the Boston area, both on TV and radio, and the place was full on the day we attended, which was in the fall, during a heavy rainstorm.

Are you getting the picture? Herb restaurants can be big draws. Lots of hard work, of course. (My husband always teased me about the garment business that I got the whole family into, with the encouraging comment that, "Well, at least you didn't get us into a restaurant. That would be even harder." But we are all dependent on restaurants, one day or another, and if that is your bent, then for heaven's sake consider an herb restaurant. For now, anyway, they can be extremely popular, gain lots of free media attention and, when run in conjunction with herb shops and gardens, be especially fine successes.

RESTAURANT REFERENCES

Starting a Small Restaurant, by Daniel Miller. Harvard Common Press, 1978.

This author loves small restaurants and their "unique role in today's stressful American society." He warns you not to listen to friends who encourage you to open a restaurant because, if you do, you'll never have a free evening to spend among friends again, and then offers you careful advice about what to do if someone falls down in the restaurant you do open. This is a very practical, thorough, and down to earth book for anyone even vaguely considering a restaurant business.

Your New Restaurant, by Vincent Mischitelli. B. Adams, New York. 1990.

How to evaluate your location, hire good help, get the word out to customers, choose a menu and convey the right atmosphere.

Pickity Place, Nutting Hill Road, Mason, New Hampshire 03048. 603-878-1151.

The Herbfarm, 32804 Issaquah-Fall City Rd., Fall City, WA 98024. 206-784-2222.

Aromatherapy

I HAVE BEEN reading about aromatherapy for quite a while, but I attended a demonstration lecture about it only recently and was amazed at the attendance. All the seats were taken in the room where the class was held so I, and several others, had to stand outside and listen at the doorway. The audience was enthusiastic and involved from start to finish during the lecture. And from what I read and hear, that is going on all over the country. Aromatherapy has arrived. It is gaining in popularity and will, I think, become a very big business in this country before very much longer.

Why? Because our noses are a direct passage way to our brains—we are very much affected by aromas. Because medical research is pointing out the effectiveness of aromas in the treatment of stress and anxiety. And because big companies are looking into the commercial applications of aroma in much the same way they took up the commercial application of music into the environment (as in Muzak—*oh, moan, groan*) years ago.

Essential oils are the basis of aromatherapy. These are the same oils that give plants their fragrance: tiny droplets of oil between the plant cells that can be extracted by several possible methods. Great quantities of the plants are required to extract small amounts of essential oils: two or three thousand pounds of roses are claimed to be required to extract one single pound of high quality rose oil. And quality, here, is really the key word. Anyone looking into the study of aromatherapy learns immediately that there are all sorts of oils in the market at many different prices. The trick is to find reputable dealers with consistently good material, and to learn a little bit about how oils are analyzed and tested.

The concentrated oils themselves are quite strong, both in aroma and chemical properties, including hormones, vitamins and antiseptics. They are almost always diluted for use as massage oils, bath oils, skin care products, and as a help towards clear thinking or getting people over depression and other emotional problems. Essential oil dispensers, usually called diffusers, are sold by aromatherapists, along with mostly blended oils for their clients' use. Aromatherapy is popular in Europe, and in France the cost of essential oils for health treatment purposes is covered by health insurance.

AROMATHERAPY REFERENCES

Supplies

Leydet Aromatics, PO Box 2354, Fair Oaks, CA 95628. 916-965-7560 FAX 916-962-3292.

Wholesale supplier of essential oils, and other aromatherapy supplies.

Original Swiss Aromatics, PO Box 6842, San Rafael, CA 94903. 415-459-3998.

Wholesale supplier of essential oils.

Aroma Vera 3384 Robertson Pl., Los Angeles, CA 90034. 310-280-0407. To order, 1-800-669-9514; FAX 310-280-0395.

Retail and wholesale aromatherapy supplies, plus home study courses and aromatherapy seminars.

Books

The Art of Aromatherapy, by Robert Tisserand. Healing Arts Press, Vermont. 1987.

This book begins with a clear explanation of essential oils, their role in the plant's life, how they are extracted, and where they come from geographically. He sees the use of essential oils as a way of reducing our dependence on chemical drugs and antibiotics, and suggests that we at least give them a chance to improve our health. Many suggestions for the use of aromatherapy in baths, massage, skin care, plus lots of recipes for combining and using the oils.

Aromatherapy Workbook by Marcel Lavabre. Healing Arts Press. Vermont 1990.

Besides a good background in the world of essential oils, this book also offers directions for extracting oils at home. Many admonitions about poor quality oils on the market and how to avoid them, plus recipes, doses, the art of blending and lots of botanical information. The author also operates a company, **Aroma Véra,** that produces, sells and distributes essential oils and other products associated with aromatherapy. They also offer seminars and aromatherapy home study courses. 5901 Rodeo Road, Los Angeles, CA 90016-4312. 310-280-0407; 800-669-9514; FAX 310-280-0395.

Aromatherapy Associations

American Society for Phytotherapy & Aromatherapy International, Inc. PO Box 3679, South Pasadena, CA 91031.

Membership: $45 and up. Quarterly journal, *Common Scents*. Send them a self-addressed stamped envelope and they will send a resource list of oil distributors, aromatherapy courses, and a book list.

National Association for Holistic Aromatherapy. PO Box 17622, Boulder, CO 80308-7622. 303-258-3791.

Membership: $35 and up. Quarterly newsletter.

Flower Remedies

NOW WE'LL TAKE yet a further step into what some will call more New Age thinking about cures, with a few references about flower remedies. Whereas aromatherapy is the inhalation of vapors of the oils from plants, flower remedies involve the ingestion of liquids secreted from flower blossoms which have been placed in water and then left in sunlight for hours. Not really an herbal subject, specifically, but flower essences are often found in herb shops and the subject is sometimes taught in herb classes. Using these flower essences in healing is an ancient tradition from India and China, but made known in modern times by Dr. Edward Bach, an English physician, now deceased. The Bach Remedies are very well known in England and research on these treatment methods is being done at the Bach Centre there. The Bach Flower Remedies are a series of 38 specific flower remedies developed and promoted by Bach and his followers.

Flower remedies are considered a branch of homeopathic medicine, where sometimes toxic ingredients are used to help trigger our bodies' defense mechanisms. Flower essences are much milder than standard homeopathic remedies, and information on flower remedies sometimes comes alongside or wrapped in other more New Age subjects, such as astrology and meditative studies. Several American companies have taken up the commercial production of flower remedies, building on the Bach list and adding many new ones. If this subject interests you, here are a few places to start a more thorough investigation.

FLOWER REMEDY REFERENCES

Ellon Bach/USA, Inc., 644 Merrick Road, Lynbrook, NY 11563.

The Bach Flower Remedies Ltd., The Bach Centre, Mt. Vernon, Sotwell, Wallingford, Oxon. OX10 OPZ, U. K.

Flower Remedies Handbook, by Donna Cunningham. Sterling Publishing Inc., New York, 1992.

This book comes with a detailed bibliography of books on flower essences and flower remedies, and a list of the companies in America that produce and sell the flower essences.

Still Other Possibilities

HERB GARDEN DESIGN AND INSTALLATION SERVICES. If you are into commercial landscape work of any kind, you can get to know herb gardening well enough to design and/or install herb gardens in your area. Almost any library book on herbs has at least one section on herb garden designs and installation. To get known in your area for such a service, volunteer to help out at any local public herb gardens, help install historical gardens at appropriate public places, or give lecture/slide shows on regional herb gardens.

HERBAL LAWN INSTALLATION and care could even be a little business. Standard green lawns that require lots of water, herbicides and pesticides, are not really the wave of the future. Herb lawns and ground covers can offer the possibility of a more natural, easy-to-care for yard.

HANGING HERBAL BASKETS

HERBAL STANDARDS

HERBAL TOPIARIES

The rest is up to you!

Books and Resources on Modern Medical Herbalism

THE FOLLOWING BOOKS and newsletters are my recommenda-tions for anyone interested in a more serious study of the plants and practice of modern medical herbalism.

Green Pharmacy, by Barbara Griggs. Healing Arts Press, Vermont, 1981.

When I first began reading about medicinal herbs, I felt lost with-out some sort of historical perspective. This book was it, for me, trac-ing from pre-history to the present, the importance of plant-based medicines and the repeated efforts to marginalize and discredit their study and use. All the important people for and against the study of medical botany; their battles, failures and successes. What a fascinating history. What a great read.

Magic and Medicine of Plants, Reader's Digest Assoc., Inc., Pleasantville, NY, 1986.

This is a reference work worth having, although not a good one for outdoor use, as it is large and fairly heavy. But for plant identification, through photographs and pleasing art work, it would be hard to beat. With one plant to the page, it gives a few paragraphs of interesting information that can help you remember each plant, plus some notes on the habitat and relevant medicinal references—both modern and historical. The first 75 pages give a grand picture of just how tightly braided is our own history with that of the plants of the earth.

Medicinal Plants of Eastern & Central North America. A Peterson Field Guide, 1991.

Written by Steven Foster and James A Duke, two of America's best known herbalists. Plant descriptions plus folk, traditional, and modern medicinal uses. An important, small format, wild-plant guide.

The Complete Medicinal Herbal, by Penelope Ody. Dorling Kindersley Ltd., London, Houton Mifflin, Boston. 1993.

This book is a feast for the eye and the mind. Ody, an English herb-alist, brings together Western, Chinese and Ayurvedic (East Indian) herbal traditions in a masterfully produced, elegant modern herbal that will probably be one of the best selling herb books ever. It brings home the important idea that the growing popularity of home health care through herbs is primarily the replacement of over-the-counter medicines—those remedies we all seek to counter the commonplace ailments that often bedevil us. The beginning of the book is a glorious full color survey of 120 medicinal herbs, showing all the plant parts that can be used, and the medicinal applications for home use. The center of the book is a home recipe section, also in full color, on the making of ointments, infusions, decoctions tinctures, etc. The last 50 pages make up the home remedy section, full of uses and dosages for many ailments, along with many cautions and precautions recommended for those trying to learn their way in simple home remedies. A remarkable book.

The Healing Herbs, by Michael Castleman. Rodale Press, 1991.

At last, a medicinal herbal for even doubting Americans: straight talk, up-front science, enthusiasm, and lots of information in easily digested blurbs and blabs. A McHerbal. I love it. Gives both the current scientific thinking on a hundred herbs, along with all possible cautionary notes, and then 200 everyday ailments herbs may help to deal with. Over 400 pages of practical medicinal herb information.

Herbal Emissaries: Bringing Chinese Herbs to the West: A Guide to Gardening, Herbal Wisdom, and Well-Being, by Steven Foster and Yue Chongxi. Healing Arts Press, Rochester, VT, 1992.

A sign of what's to come in joint efforts between Chinese and American herbalists. This book gives detailed, authoritative, and truly interesting information on the specific plants of traditional Chinese medicine. The emphasis here is on the plants themselves, and their important role as "emissaries of the medical tradition they have been a part of for thousands of years." Following a brief, fascinating introduction to the principles of traditional Chinese medicine, the book gets right to the plants: their history, characteristics, functions and uses, plus any cautionary notes about them. A full description is followed by notes on their cultivation, harvesting and processing, in both China and America. Very helpful for anyone wanting to study Chinese medicine, wanting to put in a Chinese herb garden, or wanting to grow their own medicines. An impressive accomplishment.

The Healing Power of Herbs, by Michael T. Murray, N.D. Prima Publishing, Rocklin, CA, 1992.

Written by a naturopathic doctor, with a strong emphasis on the current scientific literature about the use of thirty well known herbs and herbal formulas. Lots of organic chemistry, lots of carefully detailed explanations of the possible uses and expectations for each herb, combined with a love of and faith in botanical medicine that shines through on every page. A very special book.

Echinacea, Nature's Immune Enhancer, by Steven Foster. Healing Arts Press, Rochester, VT, 1991.

Here's a small, inexpensive paperback book that is packed with information on one important medicinal herb. It tells the history and evolution of one of the most widely used plant medicines in the world. Foster also tells how to grow echinacea and where to purchase plants and seeds. An easy read, and a perfect introduction to the whole idea of herbal medicine through one exceptionally interesting plant.

The Herbal Handbook, A User's Guide to Medical Herbalism, by David Hoffman, Healing Arts Press, Rochester, VT, 1987

A book written both for health and healing professionals and for those interested in self-care through medicinal herbs. A brief, informative history of the practice of herbalism, followed by a long reference section that lists the various actions herbs have on the body (anti-inflammatory, anti-spasmodic, etc.). There is a short herb-garden chapter on growing, drying and harvesting herbs, and then a chapter called *Herbal Pharmacy* that gives some basic recipes for making infusions, decoctions, tinctures (with alcohol, vinegar or glycerine), capsule making, bath preparations, ointments, douches, suppositories, compresses, poultices, liniments and simple oil extractions. Hoffman is English and a member of Britain's National Institute of Medical Herbalists. A later, revised edition of this book is published by Element Publishing in England, and available in the U.S. as *The New Holistic Herbal.*

Everybody's Guide To Homeopathic Medicines, by Stephen Cumming, M.D., and Dana Ullman. Tarcher Inc., Los Angeles, 1991.

Homeopathy is a medical treatment system based on the idea that "any substance which can cause symptoms in healthy people, can help to heal those experiencing similar symptoms." It uses naturally occurring chemicals (some of them quite toxic) to stimulate the body's defense systems. Though beyond the scope of ordinary herbal medicine (although it does include the use of some herbs), homeopathy is becoming so popular that I wanted to list a book that covers the subject in an accessible, intelligent way. I think this book is both a good introductory guide, and a practical use guide for those interested in this increasingly well known self-care health system.

American Herbalism: Essays on Herbs and Herbalism by Members of the American Herbalist Guild. Crossing Press, Freedom, CA, 1992.

A cross-section of some of America's most active and prolific herbalists, all writing in support of a strong, scientifically based, herbal health care system.

The New Age Herbalist by Richard Mabey. Gaia Books Ltd., London, 1988, Macmillian Publishers, NY.

One of the few books I have found that gives the actual chemical constituents of herbs. An authoritative and complete "glossary" with both drawings and color photographs for identification, showing the parts of the plant used, the main uses, the constituents and any cautions about the herb. This is followed by a fine recipe section for everything from elderflower fritters, to night cream, to herb beer. The Herbs for Healing section is a serious, yet friendly introduction, with brief overview of herbal medicine, followed by a specific list of treatments for a wide range of common ailments. Almost three hundred pages of informative, interesting herbal information. A good reference.

The Way of Herbs, by Michael Tierra. Simon and Schuster, NY, 1980. Also available in pocketbook.

Herbal medicine based on the Yin/Yang balance theory of the Orient and East Indian Ayurvedic systems. A strong section on diet with the nutritional ideas that are now becoming mainstream, but were considered so weird only a few years ago. Emphasis on the medicinal value of even the herbs in our kitchen cabinets, and then longer sections on western and Chinese herbs, and their specific uses. Includes recipes for making herbal formulas: poultice, eyewash, tonic, salve, etc. A very popular book.

OTHER RESOURCES

Globalherb, from Falcor, 5831 S Highway 9, Felton, CA 95018. 408-335-9011.

Library of medicinal herbal information for personal computers, including Macs. I have not seen this program, but the business owner, Steve Blake, offers a virtually free demonstration program. $5 covers shipping and handling.

Foster's Botanical and Herb Reviews, $8 yr. PO Box 106, Eureka Springs, AR 72632.

A quarterly newsletter that covers herb book releases around the world, written by herbalist Steven Foster.

The Herb, Spice & Medicinal Plant Digest, $8 yr. Lyle Craker, Dept. of Plant & Soil Sciences, Univ. of Mass., Amherst, MA 01003.
Gathers and reviews herbal news from around the world.

The Herbal Rose Report, by Jeanne Rose. $20 per year, 8 issues.
A new newsletter from a long experienced herbalist. Covers both medical and aromatherapy uses of herbs, plus much more.

Index

ORDER FORM

QTY	TITLE	PRICE	TOTAL
	Flowers for Sale (225 pages)	*$14.95*	
	Profits from Your Backyard Herb Garden (120 pages)	*$10.95*	
	Herbs for Sale (256 pages)	*$14.95*	
	Subtotal		
	Postage and handling (add $1.50 for one book, 50¢ for each additional book)		
	Sales tax (WA residents only, add 7%)		
	Total Enclosed		

I understand that I may return any books for
a full refund if not satisfied.

YOUR NAME _____

ADDRESS _____

CITY _____

STATE _____ ZIP _____

DAYTIME PHONE _____

☐ Enclosed is my check payable to San Juan Naturals, or
☐ Please charge my   ☐ MasterCard   ☐ Visa

ACCOUNT NO. _____

EXP. DATE _____ SIGNATURE _____

Mail or fax to: San Juan Naturals
P.O. Box 642P
Friday Harbor, WA 98250
Phone 206-378-2648   Fax 206-378-2584

If this is a library book, please photocopy this page.

Thank you for your order!